The Obstacle Course

Lessons about Business, Personal Growth and Grabbing the Brass Ring

George Lovato, Jr.

<u>Disclaimer</u>

Although this is a true story, the names of most people in the narrative have been changed. Terry, Coach Brown, Ben, Bill, Gino, Ken, Dave, Phyllis, Joe, Raul, Andy, Scotty, Bob and Tom are the actual names of real people. Other names have been changed and often represent a composite of several people into one character. This story unfolded in the early and mid 1980's. Although these events transpired decades ago they remain relevant to today's world.

ISBN 978-0-9845079-0-0

Printed and bound in US by Lightning Source

First Edition published in 2010 by Simon Cook Thinkers Press, LLC

621 17th Street
19th Floor
Denver, Co 80293

Web site: www.obstaclecoursebooks.com
                 www.buyobstaclecoursebooks.com
E-mail: george@obstaclecoursebooks.com

For purchase information or to provide feedback, or ask questions, please write to the publisher or visit the website: www.obstaclecoursebooks.com

To schedule a 30 minute live motivational presentation by Mr. Lovato call (505) 265 5123.

Dedication

I have been blessed with a wife that trusted me, a family that believed in my visions and close friends that shared my enthusiasm. I have taken many risks during my varied career. Some of these ventures are the trophies you mount on your memories wall and look back on fondly, from time to time. The failures are experiences you add to your personal textbook, try not to repeat, and pass along to others as advice for their benefit. My family allowed me the opportunity to risk, prosper, fail, learn and chart a path through my own "Obstacle Course." I am a very lucky man. Thanks!

Table Of Contents

Preface

Over the last twenty-five years scores of people have asked me what the secret is to starting your own business. My response is always the same: there are no secrets! Everyone thinks that there is something mystical about the startup process. The truth of the matter is this: anyone with the desire can begin the process. In the end, what separates the successful from the unsuccessful is one very simple ingredient: tenacity. There is nothing mystical about tenacity. Either you already possess the necessary tenacity, or you learn how to develop the tenacity needed to begin your own business.

In my career as an entrepreneur tenacity has been my primary tool. My success has been achieved because this tool, tenacity, which brings a firm resolve, persistent drive and often downright stubborn doggedness to the task at hand, has been in continuous use. Tenacity is used in combination with the second most important tool in the entrepreneur's kit: the inner voice or, as I like to call it, our gut instinct. Tenacity and gut instinct are a powerful and potent combination.

Starting a business is comparable to running an obstacle course. The first obstacles on this course include: startup financing, understanding and generating cash flow, personnel management, and clientele development and maintenance. Entrepreneurs have to be good multi-taskers. Each business will have unique obstacles that present themselves along the way, but the overcoming of these obstacles will be the same for all businesses. Knowing that there will be obstacles along the way is the first step towards a successful business startup.

You cannot know the precise nature of each of the obstacles on your entrepreneurial course, but there are steps you can take that will prepare you for some of the more common challenges. In the chapters that follow we will review these common obstacles and their solutions. Some obstacles may cause you to doubt your business abilities, and to question your decision to commit yourself to such a consuming and even risky venture. This is when tenacity and its partner, the inner voice or gut instinct, become the most valuable tools of the entrepreneur's trade.

In the narrative that follows I have attempted to share my early adventures and misadventures as a young, inexperienced entrepreneur in a format that is accessible and informative. It is my hope that my story, told in an informal, conversational style will give those considering the startup of a business encouragement and guidance. Even decades after my first venture into the world of business I certainly do not know it all. This book simply relates the ups and downs, stops and starts, reversals, leaps, falls, stumbles and victories I encountered on the obstacle course that was my first foray into the world of entrepreneurialism. Perhaps what I have learned along the way will help you to better prepare for and overcome the challenges that emerge on your particular journey.

*Remember: something drove you to consider becoming an
entrepreneur and to attempt the obstacle course and startup
of a new business in the first place. As you approach the
decision to attempt this challenge, let your tenacity maintain
and guide your commitment, and then listen to your inner
voice every step of the way. They will never fail you as long
as you ask and listen before you act, and then continue
to ask and listen and adjust your actions throughout the
process.*

1

The Decision Process and Your Inner Voice

Starting your own business is an exciting and challenging adventure. As you will learn from my experiences in this book and from your own experiences, starting and running your own enterprise is very much like participating in an obstacle course that leads you through numerous barriers and difficulties. Some of these obstacles are easy and are overcome very quickly. Others require multiple attempts in order to proceed ahead on the course. Still other obstacles call on inner strength, tenacity, faith and even just plain luck to be successfully completed.

A physical obstacle course requires upper and lower body strength as well as intellectual endurance as it tests our mental toughness and individual resolve to stay the course. The obstacle course I speak of in this book – starting and maintaining your own business – will similarly engage and test all aspects of your mental and physical capacities. As an entrepreneur you must be strong in mind and body. You must have spiritual strength. The obstacles will be numerous and the strength of your commitment to your venture will keep you on course even when it becomes rough and tough.

Hitting the Mental Gym

Just as you must train to attempt an athletic obstacle course, you must train to compete on the entrepreneurial obstacle course. You plan and prepare. You research, and then improve and amend your plan as you move through the course. This experience is a fluid and dynamic process, and flexibility is the key. You prepare for every possible obstruction and difficulty by expecting the unexpected.

My first experience in business was as a very young man. I was interested in the rental car industry and went to the local library and found every possible bit of information available on the subject. I learned that there was a ton of industry data but little to no information about how to open a rental car business. I began to talk to the franchised auto dealers in the area that had rental car operations and quizzed them about how to get started. When the library (or nowadays the Internet) is not sufficient go directly to the source. You will be surprised how cooperative people can be about assisting in your quest for information. Include retired professionals in your information quest: I often found a retiree was the best resource for startup information since they had the time to share their expertise.

During the process of seeking and gathering data and information you begin to study and familiarize yourself with the trade or business. Remember when you were in school and studied for tests? This part of the entrepreneurial process is very similar to preparing for exams. Except in this process we are studying and accumulating knowledge and information that will enable us to make a personal strategic plan. This plan is the training program that will prepare you to startup your new business.

After you have outlined a training program and plan, it's time to sit back and evaluate your commitment to this plan. Is starting up this business what you really want to do? Are you prepared to put in the hours, weeks, months, possibly years of time and energy necessary to get this business successfully on its feet? Are you prepared to make a long-term commitment to this venture?

If the answer to these questions is yes, you must next determine if your family and significant others understand and support your intention to begin this new venture. If they do support you one hundred percent you must then consider how your business will affect their lives, and talk about it with them. This is not a decision that should be made overnight. Give everyone, including you, time to digest the specifics of the plan, and discuss how the new business will impact the individual and collective home environment.

Many, if not most entrepreneurs really have no idea how much their decision to startup a business is going to affect the lives of the people around them. The decision must actively involve the people who will be affected by your commitment to the new business. Never approach their opinions about this decision in a cavalier manner. Your life and the others you love can be dramatically affected.

In my case I talked at length with my wife about my thoughts to begin my own entrepreneurial venture. For weeks we reviewed and discussed my ideas and evaluated every aspect of my initial plan's risks over and over again. I wanted my wife to be one hundred percent certain she could support my decision because this new venture was going to change her life as much as it was going to change mine.

This review process took place before I decided on the exact type of business I wanted to get into. I simply shared my entrepreneurial intentions with my wife so that she would have the opportunity to contemplate how she really felt about us taking such a big risk. After a few weeks of honest, unpressured discussion my wife agreed that it was time for me to venture out and try my hand at being the boss of my own company. She was very supportive through what would prove to be several years of the most challenging, difficult and ultimately most rewarding experience of our lives.

Reading the Map You Have Drawn

My experience taught me that the best way to approach the decision to begin a business is to map out your thoughts and strategies, and immediately share this preliminary plan with your family. It is also helpful at this stage to engage the input of a friend who has had experience with a business, and who can give you feedback about your process.

Your map should begin with a list of events that need to take place, and an outline of the fundamental elements and criteria necessary for your business to be successful. Next make a list of the events and elements that could prevent your business from being successful. Weigh them carefully. Discuss and review solutions to the obstacles on your list. Identify the solutions to successfully overcome the obstacles on your course. There may be several obstacles you do not yet know how to overcome. That's okay! Read on.

Review your two lists and weigh them again. This part of the process allows you to more fully evaluate the risks involved in your decision. Consider this exercise the rough sketch of the business plan that is made before the final blueprint. Spend some time viewing this sketch from all sides. Make a cause and effect map that identifies what needs to be done in order for you to be successful.

You will want to spend considerable time pondering the possible circumstances and elements that can hinder or complicate the course you are embarking upon. In this part of the process approach your plan from a different angle. In essence you now review the plan from the outside looking in. You become the devil's advocate. I have always been an optimist, and this kind of negative thinking was not a normal or pleasant activity for me. Considering possible disasters, stumbling blocks and failures is just out of character for me. But looking ahead and attempting to forecast the outcome of a business venture necessitates that we ponder the negative "what-if?" scenarios.

After I had made my list of goals and expectations I engaged in an evaluation exercise that acknowledged everything that I expected to happen. I then asked "What are the things that could prevent me from achieving that expectation?" I made a list of all my goals and what could prevent each of them. This process forced me to look at my plan from a more objective and global perspective. All of this assessment and evaluation is very helpful because if we only consider the positives of our plan we do not prepare ourselves for the nitty-gritty challenges of the upcoming obstacle course.

Preparing the Personal Budget

Presumably, you have already pondered the specifics of how you will support yourself and your family during the beginning stages of your new business. If not, do so immediately!

To establish a budget for the startup period of your new business, first determine the minimum dollar amount you can afford to draw from the new enterprise, if at all, in order to meet your personal financial obligations. Determine what you and your family require to live comfortably. Ask:

Can we maintain our usual standard of living, or do we need to tighten our belts during the startup of this new venture? If we must temporarily downsize, is my family willing to sacrifice some of their comforts along with me? How long can we maintain a scaled down lifestyle? What will be the fall back plan if growth of the business is slower than projected? What is the backup plan and how quickly can I implement it if the business fails? What are the cumulative risks for all involved?

These questions are important and must be considered before you proceed in your venture. This is a decision that ultimately affects many more people than just you. A new business is stressful enough without additional personal stress at home. You must be considerate of the needs of others in this process.

Organize your thoughts and plans on this matter in a detailed format. Prepare a personal financial spread sheet with every monthly obligation. Remember family expenses increase and decrease with the seasons, and certain expenses rise and fall during certain parts of the year. Insurance, utilities, auto repair and home maintenance vary but you should already know your household's trends. Really think through your situation and responsibilities as you assemble this budget. For our home I prepared a twenty-four month personal budget. It was pretty easy because I did not have very many financial obligations at the time. Little did I realize that twenty-four months would only represent the tip of the startup iceberg.

Responding to the Wisdom of the Inner Voice

You must plan for all contingencies, think of others, make a personal budget and study the obstacle course from all sides before plunging in. All of this adds up to sound thinking, right? Right. But all of this sound thinking and practical planning ought to be driven and steered by that intangible quality that prompted you to embark on this adventure course called a startup business in the first place: your inner voice, your gut instinct. Your intuition. Throughout your practical assessment and reassessment, after you have made your lists of pros and cons, evaluated your budget, determined the risks, discussed your venture with family and friends, if everything is looking solid and holding true the inner voice will persist with one blunt message: make the leap of faith.

Good business people learn to take guidance simultaneously from their rational mind and their inner intuitive voice, a.k.a., their gut instinct. Gut instinct can direct you to avoid financial and personnel disasters, and show the way to sound decisions.

Throughout the years I've spent as a businessperson and entrepreneur my gut instinct has directed me along the route and facilitated my choices during my life's journey. With my inner voice leading the way my first impressions and evaluations of risks and opportunities have most always been right and true. My intuitive first impressions of people have never been wrong.

I was a twenty-three year old kid when I started my
first business. I didn't know it at the time, but my inner
voice served me very well. I was given some advice by
a man named Bill. Bill had been very successful in the
rental car business, and he encouraged me to start a
small, independent car rental operation. I did have some
experience in the automotive industry – my father and I
had a title and registration company – and my gut instinct
said Bill knew what he was talking about. So, urged by my
inner voice to lean into this venture, over the course of a
few weeks I listened intently as Bill told me how a car rental
company works. Bill had the experienced-based information
about the rental car business I had not been able to find on
my own. Although I was completely new to the field Bill
believed I had the "right stuff" to get into the business for
myself. I had already done some preliminary research on
the rental car business and Bill was now confirming my
intuitive sense that this was a good business fit for me.

When I first shared the rental car business idea with my
wife her inner voice affirmed the idea from the start. Now,
armed with Bill's expert advice, my wife's support, and
the encouragement of my gut instinct, I went to seek the
financing needed to get the business started. I visited with
my banker, Ben, and shared with him the details of my car
rental venture. I don't know what his gut instinct was telling
him about a twenty-three year old asking for two hundred
and fifty thousand dollars, but the look on Ben's face was
not indicative of inner voice support!

Ben had some immediate concerns about the scheme:

even if I managed to get the business off the ground, Ben believed the "big guys" – the national car rental franchises – would drive me right out of business. Ben thought I was foolish not to first purchase a competitive franchise. I really believed differently. My research said that a small independent rental car company could in fact do well in my little city.

Ben then explained that the bank needed a business plan to seriously consider my proposal. I returned to the drawing board and after putting together my first and hopefully worst of my career business plan, I gave it to Ben who took my request to his loan committee. I spent the next two weeks wringing my hands as I waited to hear back from Ben and the bank. Finally, I got the call. Ben brought me in to his office, sat me down and told me, again, that I needed to think about the viability of the rental car business long and hard. I told him that I had. My inner voice was still supporting my effort. I wanted to open my own rental car business.

Convinced of my resolve, the bank decided that I could borrow about half of what I had requested. I also had to put up my house to secure the loan. I learned a lot during this first loan request: the bank was at its loan limit, and I had zero money of my own in the deal itself. In other words, no pure capital was infused in the startup operation. My business was comprised of all debt.

I risked my own home in favor of getting a loan. My bank loan constituted only half of what I needed to start the

business so I was undercapitalized. And since I was already
at the bank's loan limit, I could not ask for additional
money. I was over leveraged, and with little or no training
or experience, was about to go into the most cutthroat and
competitive business on earth – without the security of
a franchise. Why do it? My inner voice kept leading me
along. My intuition said to take a leap of faith.

One of my dearest friends at the time, Terry, learned of my
plans and wanted to join me as a partner. I needed someone
in the business like Terry whom I regarded as one of the best
salesmen in the world. I took him on as a partner. Needless
to say my father was a little hurt that I did not invite him,
too, along for the startup ride. I did not like hurting my
father's feelings, but I had my reasons. I will talk about
these later and illustrate how fluid the startup experience can
be as unforeseen needs are identified and new opportunities
emerge.

I needed more than the bank had given me to start the
business so I sought out the help of another banker friend,
Pat. Pat knew me from the registration and title business
I had with my father. Pat evidently shared my gut instinct
about the opportunity of a small car rental business because
after I outlined my vision, Pat lent me one hundred and
twenty-five thousand dollars! This loan meant I could
acquire the additional cars needed for the operation.

Although my scenario might make it seem that borrowing
money for a startup venture is easy, let me make it very clear
that financing is the single most difficult task undertaken by

any new business. For reasons I will never fully understand, what should have been the most difficult step on my first obstacle course was the easiest. The initial financing just fell together.

The fact that the financing had gone so smoothly gave me confidence and fueled me to advance quickly through the next steps. I leased a large undeveloped lot that could accommodate the business office and the rental cars' parking lot. Next I needed an ad in the Yellow Pages. Simple enough, right? Wrong! This is where I hit my first major challenge on the obstacle course. An ad in the Yellow Pages is absolutely fundamental to the success of a rental car company. This ad generates the majority of all rental car reservations, and is the single most important component in the development of clientele for an independent rental car company. Period. And here is where my inexperience became an obstacle: I was so caught up in the process of finding and building office space, installing plumbing and electrical, designing and putting up signage and fencing that I just could not be bothered with such an "inconsequential" detail as advertising. And because of my ignorance and inattention I missed the deadline for an ad in the new edition of the local Yellow Pages!

Damn the torpedoes! Full speed ahead! In August of 1982, without an ad in the Yellow Pages, (and remember this is before the world of the Internet!) I opened the doors of my little rental car business. For the first week or so of business, the telephone was absolutely silent. I stared out at the back lot admiring my fine fleet of thirty-six cars,

none of which were going anywhere. I realized it was time
to be flexible; I had to revise my plan through the obstacle
course because I had stalled out. I went out and visited
with other rental car companies and auto dealerships whose
owners I knew because they were clients of my father's
vehicle registration and title business. I asked these owners
if they would give me their overflow business. I suggested
that when they ran out of cars, I could rent my cars to their
customers at the rate they had promised. This plan worked.
I soon began to rent cars off my lot on a steady basis.

At least my business wasn't completely stalled. I knew,
however, if I was going to grow my new venture I still
needed that ad in the Yellow Pages. I was just a little local
rental car company and that singular ad was the lifeblood of
the local and regional industry. If no one knew my business
existed, no one was going to call me for a vehicle.

I remained flexible and put my ear to the ground for
opportunities. About two months after I opened a nationally
known car rental company announced it was about to close
their doors locally. They were located just up the street
from our new location, and they were also customers of my
father's title business. The manager of the operation was a
pretty good guy and he called me when he received the news
from his corporate offices that his franchise was closing. His
company had an existing ad in the Yellow Pages, and there
was an opportunity to make a deal and buy their telephone
number. The local franchise owner agreed, and this deal
finally enabled our rental car company to be listed in the
Yellow Pages. As soon as the number was transferred to our

office our phone started ringing off the wall, and we began to have customers of our very own.

I had listened to my inner voice when it came to making Terry my partner. I knew he was a skilled salesman. I knew he would add value to the enterprise. One of the important facets to growing a local car rental company is to obtain month to month or long term contract business. My partner, Terry, being a super salesman, was able to hit the streets and capture this type of business. He was a whiz. People liked him. Terry had a professional appearance and made a skilled presentation. He was comfortable talking to the big Fortune 500 companies and brought us results very quickly. This stabilized our revenues and we began to measure profits. Our competitors, as well as our banker, Ben, were surprised by our rapid growth.

Terry contributed to the early success of the business. He was an excellent choice for a partner, but he was also my best friend. This is not always a wise choice: it is best to be cautious about making your best friend your partner. There can be many problems associated with going into business with a friend or a member of your family. Later in the book I will talk at length about some of the rules to follow when starting a business with friends and family.

When I was considering Terry as my partner my inner voice was affirming this action and telling me to move forward. There have been other times when the inner voice has told me to stop. I have not always followed intuitive directions, or have chosen not to heed them. Looking back I see that when I did not follow the directions of the inner voice, mistakes occurred that led to difficulties and even failure. And in those times that I did listen to my intuition, and followed my gut instinct, I was successful. It cannot be repeated enough: listen to your inner voice and continue to monitor and evaluate your feelings with your gut instinct and intuition as you move along the obstacle course.

Getting into business for your self is a long and frequently complicated process. My first experience was very unusual. In my other business ventures the startup phase was far more difficult. The financing phase is most often long and complicated. If it were easy to finance a new business more people would undertake a venture, and less people would fail and give up. Your commitment to your new enterprise is going to be tested every step of the way. Once you start the process, you must commit and recommit yourself to the plan. Set your goals in small attainable increments and knock them off one by one. Stay focused on the immediate tasks at hand. By staying focused on the tasks in front of you the larger goal of starting your business will be achieved.

The day to day tasks involved with running the business demand constant attention. Sales, cash and customer flow, frequency of calls and business eventually fall into a predictable tempo. When this tempo or rhythm begins to stutter and misfire you need to recognize and respond to the change. You monitor the daily rhythm of your business and adjust operations so that they maintain an even pace. Pay close attention to daily details. Your gut instinct can steer you through the ebb and flow of a new business, and help you establish the best tempo to keep your momentum moving in a forward direction.

During those first months of startup I was working fourteen and eighteen hour days. The energy and excitement of the new business kept me going; time was just not a factor. I was having a ball! It seemed natural to pour this much time into the new venture. The days turned into weeks; the weeks turned into months, and before I knew it six months had passed. I was renting cars. I was selling cars. I was making money. Work did not seem like work. Terry and I were at the office seven days a week and we were having a million laughs along the way. He had a good sense of humor and made it a point to keep things around the office light. We had hired four employees, and they all loved Terry as did our customers. Terry was a real asset, and was a major contributor to the good rhythm and vibe surrounding the new business.

Choosing great partners and good employees is critical to the success of your business. Selecting your partner early on in the startup process is imperative. This person needs to be someone you trust and also someone with whom you will be able to work long hours. A partner's skills should complement your skills. One person cannot be expected to overcome all obstacles. Consider who you need and want for your partner(s) carefully. These are the people who will help to make or break your business. In the chapters to come you will see how a partner's role, contributions and value to the business can change over time.

Chapter Summary

Often it seems that the decisions involved in the startup process can be overwhelming. Ironically, if you are involved with this process in the manner that it demands it will overwhelm you. Each of the decisions involved during startup are an essential part of the test or screening process. If you cannot make it through this part of the obstacle course then what is to come will certainly beat you. Are there any short cuts? No! Making a plan, identifying resources and partners, securing financing and accessing risks as the whole process unfolds are all too important to the success of the business to warrant any short cuts. Give more time not less to the decision process because you never get another chance to view the course from afar and with 360 degree glasses.

In retrospect I should have spent more time planning and thinking about all the potential obstacles in my first business venture. I would have been much more successful had I taken more time to evaluate all the potential factors to the business' success or potential failure. But I was young, impetuous and invincible! Over time I would find that being young was an obstacle in itself. I would also find that my impetuous nature, at times an asset, was too often a major liability. Ultimately I would discover that I was not invincible but was in fact quite vulnerable.

There is no magic to the process of starting a business. You must research your venture. Your must prepare a personal plan and prepare yourself for each step of that plan. You must commit to your venture with your heart and mind, and make sure your family understands and supports your commitment. And most importantly you must listen to your inner voice and follow the guidance offered by your intuition. If there is only one morsel of advice you take away from this chapter it is to listen to the inner voice. It will never lead you astray.

2

Visualization:
The Importance of Seeing it in Your Mind

When I was young I was always involved in athletic activities. From football to track to golf and tennis, as a child I was constantly trying to learn a new game or sport. As I got older I began to play only those sports I was better at; in a sense I became more selective. My drive to excel pushed me to practice even after practice was over, shooting baskets at home, lifting weights and pursuing various strength building or skill improving activities. I reached a point in junior high where I did not seem to improve at all. I just sort of stagnated. Enter Coach Brown. Brown was an athletic, energetic guy who did everything well. I admired him and thought he was a great coach and person.

Visualizing Success: Seeing the Whole Game

One day I spoke with Coach Brown about how I was not improving as a receiver in football. He told me I had all the physical skills and coordination needed to be a good receiver but that I lacked a different kind of skill. A mental skill. Coach Brown said I needed to learn how to visualize. Before I came to practice or even went onto the field I needed to imagine catching the ball or running a certain type of pattern in my mind first. Once I could see it in my mind, come practice or game time, running a pattern and catching the ball would just be second nature.

At first I did not understand what the coach was saying. Brown guided me through the steps of visualization. He told me to start from the beginning and imagine the whole game in my mind first; to follow the game in my head as if I was watching a movie of myself. Then he instructed me to take those visions and transform them into the real thing when I played the game. All of a sudden a light bulb went on in my head. Coach Brown was talking about mental practice. From then on, before each game I would sit in a quiet place and let the entire game unfold in my mind, imagining exactly how I would successfully execute each play. My skills improved and I started catching more passes and scoring touchdowns.

Today this mind-body concept of personal development is a widely accepted practice, and sport psychologists specialize in teaching the techniques and coaching athletes in the mental game. But not so thirty years ago. Coach Brown was a man before his time. Visualization was just coming into vogue among professional athletes. About the same time Coach Brown was telling me about visualization, the American Olympic teams were applying the same method to just about every sport. The mental game was especially employed by downhill skiers. I had begun to ski and a ski racing coach I had at the time was preaching the benefits of the mental game, visualizing the race course before stepping into the starting gate. I began to use creative visualization in just about every activity I was participating in. My skiing techniques improved and I was able to compete with faster, better athletes. I did not understand exactly how visualization worked but I could see the results in a very real way.

I was too young to care, but the physical success I was getting from mental visualization could actually be scientifically explained. Modern study of the brain has revealed that ninety percent of the brain's sensory stimulation is triggered by visual information. The brain reacts most quickly to visual stimuli – color, motion, form and depth. The brain has an attention bias for stimuli with high contrast and novelty, and also has an immediate and primal response to symbols. We are a visual being and most of us better remember what we see than what we read or hear.

Mental Imaging: Harnessing the Power of Daydreams

So exactly what is visualization? Often called creative visualization, many practitioners consider it a form of active, directed daydreaming. Some call it mental imaging. Others call it a mental rehearsal. Many people who use it regularly consider it a form of meditation. For the purposes of this book I just call it visualization. Basically, we create with our imagination exactly what we want in our life. Our mind's eye acts as a movie projector of sorts and casts images of our goals, intentions and aspirations onto our brain, into our memory.

There are several methods and systems available for developing this skill. (See the Further Reading section at the end of the book.) However, there are some common steps used by people who routinely and successfully practice visualization. The first step is to create an idea of what we want. Then we mentally build upon that idea, giving it depth and detail, creating images that support the goal, and give the vision power in our mind and in our emotions. We give our dream form. And since form guides energy, we then begin to move towards manifestation of our visualization.

Maybe you're not sure you can imagine your ideas and dreams taking form; or if you are even capable of active creative daydreaming. The following exercise will take you through the basic steps of active visualization.

Take a moment to look around your immediate environment with your eyes open. For the next two minutes study the room you are in and view the details of your physical surroundings. Now close your eyes. Is it the room you have just studied that you see? It can be. But perhaps you notice that other inner images begin to form. Your imagination will take you beyond the physical reality you are part of in the room and begin to manifest and project other forms and symbols into your awareness. Notice how these projected forms and images are viewed by your inner eyes as easily as the physical room around you just viewed with your outer eyes. These inner images merge into your mind where they are experienced exactly as the images seen in the physical world, and also produce emotions and memory. Now try focusing on something you want in your life. Be very clear. Call images to your mind's eye that embody what you want. Feel it, see it in your life now. In your imagination, manifest your dreams into form. You are a powerful creator.

This is a simple demonstration of the brain's imaginative powers. These inner images, although not part of the physical environment you have just studied in the room around you, are equally real to your mind's eye. People may not attach very much importance to the inner images they create and imagine but they are very powerful within the brain and emotions.

The scientists involved with quantum physics have concluded that our thoughts have a mighty influence on our physical reality. I cannot say I understand quantum physics but my own experiences with the mind-body connection and my successful use of visualization techniques in daily life have brought me to my own non-scientific conclusion: visualization works.

Remember the old saying that "seeing is believing"? Meaning, we must see it first in order to believe it. That old adage is being enhanced by new theories based on scientific research related to quantum physics. The new theory suggests that we can create and see the reality we want to move towards in our mind first. With a clear image of our intentions held firmly in our mind's eye, we then begin to mentally create and bodily move towards the reality physically. What we envision is in fact what we will manifest. There it is: visualization in a nutshell.

It goes without saying (although I am going to say it!) that it is important to our health and well being that our visualizations focus upon and maintain positive intentions. If we focus upon a view of the world and our activities upon it with uplifting and encouraging imagery and intentions then that will be our outcome. However, if we view ourselves and our world through negative eyes and visions, then that will be our reality. So choose to visualize only through a positive lens. When you imagine your business, always project and visualize positive, successful images in your mind's eye. Imagine the best that can happen, always.

The generating of this optimistic inner movie should be an ongoing, repetitive practice. I found that when I was under a good deal of stress visualization became as a relaxation technique. Today everyone is talking about and using visualization. This is because it does work. It has become a common and accepted daily practice for athletes, health providers, and business owners. Make positive visualization a daily practice.

Visualization and Focus: Life as a Movie

At the startup of my first business years had passed since my days with Coach Brown and I had forgotten all about the benefits of visualization. I was totally focused on getting the ball rolling in my new venture, but was not using any of the visualization techniques that had helped me as an athlete. I needed to be reminded.

When the word got out I was going to start a rental car company one of my good friends, Gino, was enthusiastic and encouraging. He was in the automotive industry and was very successful at the time. Gino gave me a lot of advice with startup. He sat me down and advised me about who to do business with and who to stay away from insofar as buying the cars needed for our fleet. During one of our conversations Gino suggested that if I wanted to be successful with my new venture I needed to imagine all that I wanted to achieve in my mind first. He said, "See it like a movie."

I was thunderstruck! A flash went off in my head and I remembered Coach Brown and visualization. Here I was years later with a business associate, Gino, reminding me about the benefits of visualization. I began visualizing again every single day. I visualized my logo. I visualized my location. I visualized the fleet of cars and seeing an empty lot rather than a full one. Over the next months as the business came together the outer reality developed just as I had seen it in my inner reality. And the actual process and practice of daily visualization kept me focused, positive and calm. I was under a lot of stress and the daily practice was a sedative to my system. After fifteen or twenty minutes of visualizing I felt noticeably more relaxed and was able to retain my focus and calm during very stressful days. Thanks to Gino I was reminded of a very important skill I learned when I was young.

Visualization and Obstacles

Visualization kept me in a positive frame of mind during the stressful startup period of my new business. The obstacles encountered were less overwhelming when I began to visualize their solutions. It seemed somehow both amusing and appropriate that something I had learned as kid in sports was also useful as an adult in business.

In retrospect I think one of the reasons the major difficulties I encountered on my first obstacle course did not discourage me or cause me to give up was because I had held such positive images in my mind about what I was attempting to accomplish. I held the image of successful completion front and center throughout the startup process.

As I mentioned earlier, when I received the news that I had missed the deadline for the Yellow Pages ad, I just kept moving forward. I was visualizing that I was renting cars and so I did not imagine that not having an ad was going to present a problem. Naïve, yes, but I was positive about finding a solution! I was visualizing solutions. Perhaps this is why I responded so quickly to the opportunity to buy the telephone number connected to the Yellow Pages ad from my competitor. I was visualizing a solution to getting the word out about our new car rental business in my mind's eye and when the solution emerged, I was ready. I acted quickly and this allowed me to move forward faster than I had anticipated.

As time passed the fleet of rental cars expended to meet the needs of our growing customer base. At one point we had a considerable number of trucks, vans and 4x4's. Every day we were getting busier and busier. It was at this point I began to visualize bigger things. I did not like the extreme fluctuations in the reservation schedule. We needed a more consistent level of rentals day to day, week to week. I began to research how the big guys generated their reservations and discovered that the airline industry and travel agents controlled the number and frequency of their car rentals. Additionally I learned that getting linked into the travel reservation business would be a huge investment. But I could see that generating reservations from travel agents and airlines could be a significant boom to our existing business.

The Gut Instinct and Visualization

I shared my idea about linking our reservations with travel agents with my partner Terry. Terry's initial reaction was that I was nuts. Terry did not think such an arrangement was even possible. But I explained that if we wanted the rental business to grow we needed to be in the reservation business. Terry asked how we could even consider this in light of the fact that it was going to take big money to even get the reservation system started. I then began to verbally lay out a plan whereby we would sell reservations to other independent car rental companies from the airline reservation systems generated from the travel agents and also through an 800 number. This added revenue would defray the costs of setting up a system by ourselves. In essence we would form a coalition of independent operators and become something like the Best Western of the car rental business. Terry shook his head in disbelief. It was a big plan, but Terry did not argue very long against this idea. After all, he and I had come this far together. And Terry also knew by now that I had a tendency to follow my intuitions and my gut instinct. Like me, he was learning to trust those instincts.

I told Terry how I could see the entire venture in my head beginning with what we needed to build a reservation operation and continuing through to how we would sell this concept to other independent car rental companies. Terry kept saying over and over how he thought it could not be done. I kept saying I was visualizing the whole thing so we were okay. At this point I think he thought he ought to call in the guys with the white coats and have me put away until I got over this delusion. But being a good partner meant that he at least listen and hear me out, and he did.

I began the process of putting my plan down on paper. I did a considerable amount of investigation on the car rental reservation systems and talked to countless people in the airline business. I spoke with scores of travel agents about how they connected clients to plane, hotel and rental car reservations. Over the course of about three months I put a plan together that illustrated in detail how I was going to develop a national network of independent rental companies that would function as a cooperative linked through a single shared reservation system. The information and the plan came together very quickly and we soon had a blue print for how we would get the airlines to supply the connections to their respective systems. This plan also anticipated our need to get access to and market the 800 number. But how fast even the best laid plans can be changed!

The People Quotient: Learning As We Go

During this same period of time, back at our car registration and title business, my father was running into some difficulties with the state regulators. At that time we had almost a monopoly on the type of service we were offering and the state regulators decided that maybe they needed to further regulate what we were doing. The indecision and interference of the state regulators was putting added burdens on the enterprise and on my father.

Over at the new rental car business our clientele was growing at a very rapid rate. It was soon evident that to grow, even to maintain our business base, we needed to add more cars. And quickly.

In a casual meeting one afternoon my dad told me of his professional challenges and I told him of mine. During that meeting we both realized that we really needed one another. He needed me to help him with his office's challenges, and I needed him to help me guarantee the loans for more cars.

That day I decided to talk to Terry about adding my dad as a third partner.

Terry and my dad had always gotten along very well. He knew what good friends Terry and I were, and my dad thought we would eventually wind up doing something professionally together. My dad, although hurt that he was not asked, was not surprised when Terry became my first partner. I knew Terry would most likely welcome my dad into our partnership.

I called Terry and set up a meeting with the three of us at my dad's house. At this meeting I introduced to Terry and my father a plan on how our partnership could be modified to accommodate my dad's interest. I explained how we would be able to divide up certain tax benefits available at the time. Terry was all for adding my dad as a third partner. We shook on it and the deal was done. Within the week we started to make plans to move the car rental operation into the same building that the title business was located in. This involved a good deal of remodeling but my dad took control of the construction needs and in his indomitable style had the new space ready for us to move into in just a few weeks.

From the very beginning I had the thought in the back of my mind that my dad would one day get involved in the new venture. I just didn't know exactly how. In a sense this was passive visualization. I could picture my father becoming a partner, and I could feel how this would be good for the business, but I could not yet see precisely how it would evolve.

Visualization and listening to my intuition were now working in unison. The rental car business was growing at a brisk pace and we were adding to the fleet of cars on a monthly basis. I had plans on the table to expand the operation in another direction – a national reservation system – to complement growth, and had added my father as a third partner. I could clearly visualize all the elements in my mind.

Chapter Summary

Visualization is a practice that you can incorporate into your daily professional and personal routine. It is important to visualize only positive actions and outcomes. Visualization can assist you as you form and plan your intentions, and will prepare you to meet and overcome the challenges on the course ahead. You can use visualization as a form of meditation to keep yourself focused on your goals. Visualization is a powerful ally when the obstacle course becomes particularly challenging. Visualization is a powerful tool that can benefit your business and you, personally, when practiced regularly.

3

The Right People, The Right Partners and The Professionals Around You

A successful enterprise is made up of people. Selecting the right people to be involved in your business is very important. The single most important person is your business partner. Selecting a compatible, knowledgeable partner requires much thought, and is not to be done in haste or without careful consideration of several factors that will be discussed in this chapter. When you assemble your business, besides your partner(s), associates and employees, you will also want to have a circle of experts whose advice and experience will guide your company through startup, and then continue to assist you through the on-going, day to day decision making process inherent in any business endeavor.

The People Quotient: Positive People Generate Positive Energy

The common denominator of these three factors critical to a successful business – finding the right partner(s), selecting the right people to work in your office, and assembling a circle of expert, supportive advisors – is the contribution and dynamic potential found in human interaction. Very seldom can a business exist without direct, sustained participation from a team of committed individuals. Therefore the people quotient, the human element, is among the most important components of a business's long term success.

I always surround myself with positive people. Positive people are encouraging of my endeavors, optimistic about my chances at something new, and affirm what I am doing or considering to do. This does not mean they withhold constructive criticism or are unable to express reservation or doubt about an idea or action based on their own experience. Positive, supportive people may challenge or disagree with my choices, and challenge my thinking, but they are always ultimately concerned with my business's success and my own personal well being. We all need these people in our lives and in our work.

In the case of starting the rental car company, everyone I spoke with, friends and professionals alike, were enthusiastic and supportive about me starting my own operation. In the early 1980s, being a young entrepreneur was very much in vogue. It seemed that if you were under thirty and in business for yourself, well, that was sexy and saleable. I capitalized on the prevailing social and economic climate and at twenty-three jumped into a profession with Big Names as my main competitors. What did I know? As you'll read in the next chapters, not very much! Hindsight is, of course, twenty-twenty. I guess this means that we learn a lot in our twenties!

The people around me were very encouraging of my business plan. Positive energy is powerful and energizing, and the confidence of my friends and colleagues propelled me forward at a very swift pace. All of the customers in my father's title business were enthusiastic about seeing me start this new business. I kept hearing "If you need anything or I can help give me a call." One of the clerks in the title business, Phyllis, was particularly encouraging. She repeatedly said that she thought I was ready to step out on my own, and asked everyday how I my new plan was coming along. I fed on this uplifting energy and it charged my personal battery when times were low and slow. I made sure to keep myself surrounded with people who were optimistic. They kept me thinking positively. Nay-sayers did not last long in my circle of advisors and business associates.

Can Best Friends Be Great Partners?

In previous pages I have spoken about my partner Terry. At the time of my first business enterprise, Terry was my best friend. Six years my senior, I looked up to Terry like an older brother. He was a genuinely funny and witty guy, and I could count on Terry to make any situation light-hearted.

Our wives had been close friends since junior high school, and we often socialized together as couples. In simple terms, we all got along very well.

After I had begun the startup process of the new rental car company Terry asked if he could join the venture as a partner. It seemed like a good and natural proposition. He was my best friend, but he was also a super salesman. And I really needed a salesman in the operation. Besides, I trusted Terry as if he were my own brother. I needed someone to watch my young back and he knew that I would in turn look out for his.

Terry had a college degree. He worked for the Chamber of Commerce in the Convention Bureau. His job was to encourage organizations to locate their meetings and conferences in our home town. Terry did a fantastic job and was well known in city business circles. He later moved on to pharmaceutical sales, and worked his way to the top of the company very quickly. Terry was meeting or surpassing company goals and expectations very quickly after they hired him. He was just a super salesman. People liked to be around Terry, and he used his popularity and easy-going persona to his professional advantage continually. I am sure everyone has done business with a really gifted salesman. When they sell you something you think "Wow, it's a pleasure to do business with this guy. He's really good!" Terry was that kind of guy.

A partnership is a complicated relationship. Your partner must be someone who you inherently trust, and yet the words from the wise insist that you never choose a friend to be your partner. Ironic, because who do we trust more than our closest friends? Why not take a best friend for a business partner? Thirty years of experience later, I understand why close friends as partners goes against the best business practices. But at twenty-three, I still had some wising up to do.

I knew that I needed Terry's skill set as a salesman. I needed someone who I trusted to make good, sound decisions when I was not around the business. I also needed someone who was of like mind in the way I was visualizing the future of the company. Terry was my best friend, knew how I functioned personally, and had the professional skills I needed for a partner. So what was the problem? The problem, as it would emerge farther down the road, was not in selecting Terry as my business partner. The problem was that from the beginning there were no boundaries, no rules, no defined roles and expectations. And this is where best friends who become business associates go wrong: we didn't realize that good friends need to formally, clearly redefine their relationship within a business partnership.

The Business Relationship: Defining the Roles, Setting the Boundaries

If in spite of advice against it if you decide to make a friend your business partner you must set in stone the terms of your business relationship. You must each adopt and agree upon very defined professional roles. You must set the boundaries of the business relationship and the friendship. You must articulate the goals and expectations of each partner, and have a formal set of rules that you work by. These include individual time off, separating work from your social interactions, agreeing when it is appropriate to discuss the office and the business and when it is not, and how and when to settle disputes. Friends deal with these issues in ways that are not appropriate to business associates. Terry and I did not establish these ground rules when we became partners. We just went along like usual, as friends who were now business colleagues. We were a pretty successful team when we started out, but over time our relationship would begin to deteriorate as the inevitable stresses and strains of a new business venture became the focal point of our friendship.

As I shared earlier, when I began the new business my father was a little hurt that I did not immediately ask him to join Terry and me on our new adventure. After all, my father and I had already been partners in a very successful business. There was a reason that I did not first ask my father to help with the startup: I wanted to put myself and what my father had taught me to the test, see if I could in fact run my own business. I knew that after the dust settled I would ask for his participation. But at the beginning I needed to set out on my own and test the waters by myself.

Back to the Bank: Growing a Business

Time passed and our business grew. Within nine months we had more customers than cars. I was now focused on two things: first, I was trying to get additional financing to meet the needs of the growing demand for more vehicles; and second, I was trying to figure out a way to build our own national reservation system.

It was soon clear that the need for more cars was critical. You can only turn potential customers away so many times before they do not come back. Our records demonstrated the volume of reservations we were not filling on a daily basis because of our small inventory of rental cars. We needed more money. But our business was young, and to loan officers, we did not have enough of a track record to demonstrate the success of the company to lenders. Bankers repeatedly told me that nine months of operations was not enough time to tell if the business was able to support more debt.

There is a lesson here to be learned about bankers: when you begin a business find and select bankers that do in fact understand your business. You may have to educate bankers about the ins and outs of your business before they really "get it." If you pitch your venture to a pencil pushing bank underling who does not understand your goals they will sell your business short when it comes to crunch time. I actually began the car rental business with two very good bankers, but when I approached them about additional funds, both were at their respective loan limits. There was nothing more they could do for me. These bankers did understand my business, but their institutions could not extend more credit even if they wanted to; they were at their limit.

This situation forced me to solicit loans from bankers that did not understand business in general and my business in particular. I had to deal with people who were very uninformed, and who left me wondering how such naïve loan officers served their banks at all! For example, one of these bank officers asked me if I had permission from Hertz to operate my business in Albuquerque?! Another loan officer asked me what college I attended to get my degree in car rental? This was the dismal caliber of bankers I was dealing with. After a month hearing such nonsense at meetings I was so frustrated I went to Terry and told him we were at a standstill. We were up against an obstacle that was blocking all movement. To move forward, we were going to need some financial assistance from the outside. In other words we needed another partner.

Taking on More Partners: New Opportunities, Old Problems

As explained previously, my father and Terry got along very well. When I said that we ought to talk to my father about becoming our partner, Terry was delighted. My father needed the tax breaks our little business could provide, and he was happy to finally be asked to join the team. Negotiations were straightforward and effortless, and once the partnership was official we went off to visit with my father's banker.

With a bigger financial statement – my father's – in hand, we talked with a loan officer at a bank with a large lending limit and a bank lending limit ten times the size of our existing banks, we were finally able to secure the money we needed to move forward. With this new loan we were able to pay off our startup loans with the original banks, and set up new, larger loans with our new bank. We also set up loans through one of our car dealership friends at GMAC.

New long-term rental car contracts and some additional travel broker business began to show amazing results. In addition, we soon had a new larger ad in the latest edition of the Yellow Pages. When it all hit it was like an explosion in our office! Terry could not have been happier; my father was shocked, delighted and a little taken back by this business boom. Bolstered by our success, I was ready to move on to the second part of our business' expansion – the setting up a national reservation system.

As I have stated earlier, when you take on a partner you must set boundaries. Unfortunately, I had not learned this lesson and when my father joined as a partner, the basic boundary setting was again overlooked. Trouble soon began to brew. My father wanted to put in his two cents about running the operation, and even assumed that he was or should be the boss. I saw things differently.

Daily if not hourly disagreements began to occur around the office. Terry was put right in the middle of the father-son struggle and although he tried to keep the peace, he could not. Our disagreements came to a head. In my opinion the things my father wanted to do were just not appropriate to the way the business was operating. Some of the changes he wanted to initiate we had already tried and found to be unsuccessful or unprofitable. Terry and I had already been over this ground with the business. I really believed that I knew what the business needed to succeed.

One day, in order to prove my point, I walked out of the office and left my father to run the business. It did not take long for him to see that there was a lot about running this car rental business that he did not know. Even relatively simple things for the average business – like making a deposit or paying bills – were different because of the way bank and credit card accounts were set up. It was a lesson well taken. After a few days, one of our family lawyers called and set up a meeting with everybody. My dad and I sat down and in a few short hours we resolved our differences. New boundaries and expectations were set, and the role that each of us would play in running the operation was clarified and agreed upon.

This experience was a valuable lesson. Rules, boundaries, defined roles and expectations were set. Unfortunately, it took a personal and professional crisis to accomplish this. The crisis, however, should never have happened. The rules, roles and boundaries should all have been put on the table at the outset of the partnership. And the lesson was still not entirely heeded: Terry and I had yet to define these important roles and to set boundaries between ourselves. We were still winging it. We needed to get this out on the table, but we were too busy having fun and making money. We just did not know any better. Our lack of attention about this issue would prove to be a monumental mistake.

Structure, Structure and More Structure: The Successful Business Relationship

It cannot be said enough: put the discussion about professional roles, responsibilities, boundaries and expectations on the business table at the very beginning. Ask, discuss, research these key topics and make sure your partner(s) knows what each person's role in the business is and vice versa. Clarify:

- *What does each of you expect from the other?*
- *Who is the director, chief officer, leader and/or company president?*
- *When and under what conditions do you and your partner(s) discuss business? During business hours? Never on weekends? Only at the office? And etc.*
- *And most importantly, what are the guidelines and rules that will be followed when partners need to resolve differences? Write them down.*

It would have helped our business enormously if Terry and I, and my father and I, had discussed these elements and come to an agreement during our first conversations about the venture. The disagreement and misunderstanding between my father and I would never have escalated to crisis proportions. And Terry and I would have had the necessary structure in our professional relationship to weather the events to come.

We did do one thing right: we called upon our family attorney to help us resolve differences. The input of a skilled and trusted professional during our business crisis was absolutely essential to the resolution of those differences. He was objective about the situation, and yet familiar with the players and able to understand the nuances of the conflict. Having a seasoned, smart, trusted professional such as our family attorney was a real asset to the business.

The crisis was difficult but it did produce something very positive. In the resolving of our differences everyone agreed I should focus my energy on getting the national reservation system off the ground. Both Terry and my father saw the merit in the plan I had put together. For me, this was where the real excitement in my first venture as an entrepreneur began.

Chapter Summary:

Selecting the right people to be involved in your business is critical to the success of the business. The single most important person is your business partner. Selecting a compatible, knowledgeable, positive partner requires much thought and is not to be done in haste. When you assemble your business, besides your partner, associates and employees, you will also want to have a circle of experts whose advice and experience will guide your company through startup, and then continue to assist you through the on-going, day to day decision making process inherent in any business endeavor. Choose only positive people for your business partners and associates. Seek out people who are encouraging of your endeavors and optimistic about your new company. This does not mean they are people without constructive criticism. But their overall attitude is one of beneficial, upbeat advice and support based on their own experience.

Whether or not if you, like me, decide to make a good friend your business partner at the outset of your partnership, adopt and agree upon well defined roles and terms for your business relationship. Set the boundaries of the business relationship and , if applicable, the friendship. Delineate goals and expectations and develop a formal set of rules that you both agree to work by.

4

Daily Planning, Goal Setting and Providence

After twelve months in business, the car rental venture was doing very well. We were buying cars, renting cars and selling cars. Revenues were growing, and Terry and my Dad were working well together. It was time for me to focus on the startup of the new venture – the national reservation system.

Once again I was, by choice, starting a new business about which I knew absolutely nothing. And as had been the case with the car rental enterprise there was no single source of information on how to start a national independent car rental reservation system. My experience with the first business startup did teach me something, however, and for this new business I spent time talking to people already in the industry *before* I began.

I sought out and had meetings with franchise operators and gleaned as much basic knowledge as I could about the reservation system that generated their car rental business. I met with travel agents and learned about the airline reservation system they used and how they interacted with those systems. Armed with all of this knowledge and information I began to refine my business plan. I recognized at the outset that my plan did not have a specific approach as to the selling of this scheme to other independent operators. However, I believed that after I put together the initial startup plan I would be able to formulate an additional plan to sell the system to other independent car rental enterprises.

Blue Print: The Calendar, Executive Summary & Budget

I made a list of target cities that were important links in the first phase of building the reservation system. I then created a calendar of deadlines for the startup of the system. This calendar identified and defined various tasks that had to be accomplished, and became a set of detailed outlines of various components essential to operating the national reservation business. The calendar and outline was summarized into an executive summary and budget. These twenty pages of information were my blue print to build a national car rental reservation system.

Building a Business with the Blue Print

I still needed more core data on the car rental industry. I searched library resources (remember this was a few years before the wonders of Internet research could be accessed through your personal computer!) for a few weeks but found nothing offering specific or even general information and assistance about the industry.

Serendipitously, American Express Travel released their Industry Survey. I read about the survey in the Wall Street Journal (national and regional news publications provide an on-going source of information and research, and reading these is part of an entrepreneur's daily tasks) and acquired a copy of the complete study. This survey proved to be very informative and revealing, and gave me statistics on the industry I did not know existed. The most important fact revealed in that survey was that independent car rental operators comprised a very large portion of the rental car industry. Bingo! My target market! I now understood the size and scope of my target market – independent rental car operators like me – and finally had statistics affirming our importance to the travel industry.

I formulated a plan to sell a reservation system to independent car rental operators that combined a host of related services. This was a blue print for the "Best Western" hotel system of the car rental industry. After putting together a simple presentation I obtained the Yellow Pages books for ten major western cities. I studied the ads in the car rental section and identified what appeared to be the best independent operators. With all of this information I chose the target cities for the national reservation system startup: Los Angeles, Phoenix, Las Vegas, Denver, Dallas and Houston.

I learned from the American Express Travel Industry Survey that travel agents arrange and book the vast majority of car rental reservations. I also learned that these reservations were generated through the colossal airline reservation systems. My independent car rental business needed to be listed as a choice on the airline reservation systems right alongside Hertz, Avis, National and Budget. This would be the single most important element in building this business. Just like I needed the Yellow Page ad for my startup car rental operation to be successful, this new reservation system needed to be included in the huge airline system so that travel agents could make reservations directly with our operation, and also access our network of independent car rental agencies.

 I booked a two-week trip to begin the process of selling the reservation system to one independent car rental representative in each of my target cities. We decided I would have a budget of $10,000 for airfare, hotel and meals. Armed with my business plan, supporting research and bundles of optimism, off I went to start up this new arm of our business.

Unfortunately, in my usual "buggy before the horse style" I set off on this adventure without first accomplishing several items from my blue print of key components: I did not have the 800 number for the national reservation system, the airline reservation system installed, or even the legal agreement prepared for an independent car rental company to sign in order to become our system representative in the target city! I was moving ahead of the calendar I myself had designed! I excused all of this because I felt the idea was good enough to sell using my simple presentation. I decided that I could get by without those other "minor details" in place.

First stop: Los Angeles. I talked with a dozen or so independent car rental operators. First lesson: site visits are very important when identifying potential system partners! Upon meeting with some of these owners and seeing their physical location and operations in person, I knew that I would not want to rent a car from some of these guys, so why would anyone else?! Their operations were nothing like ours. Some had beat up cars and dirty locations – certainly not the caliber of businesses we wanted to be associated with. But my site visits also revealed several really first class operations. Those were the business I wanted to link with.

I gave my simple presentation about our idea for an independent rental car system to the first targeted business and they wanted to sign on. There was only one problem: I had no agreement for them to sign! I jumped onto the phone and called the family lawyer and asked him to put a legal agreement together quickly. He responded in a few hours. (Remember the previous chapter about working with the right advisors and support team!) Our lawyer again came through for our business: he had the background knowledge of what we were doing, and was able to produce what I needed on very short notice. The agreement came through from the lawyer, and we signed on our first affiliate in the reservation system. Along with that signature, I collected a check for a few thousand dollars that represented the operator's exclusive right to represent our car rental reservation system in his city.

Off I went to Phoenix where I met a family that had been in the car business for a long time. The sons of the owner ran the car rental operation. One of the sons, Joe, was my contact. He was genuinely impressed with the overall plan and saw how the system could grow by targeting the independent operator. He also understood how the national reservation system could bring him additional business. Joe even told me that he wished he thought of it first!

With the L.A. operator already signed on it was easier getting Joe's company on board. I spent time talking with the brothers, too, explaining the plan. They eventually agreed with Joe that the affiliation would be good for their business. My last task was to convince their father. Their father wanted to do a background check on me and our business back in Albuquerque. This was fine with me and demonstrated to me that theirs was a quality business. The father made several phone calls to car dealers in Albuquerque asking about our professional reputation and business practices. Everything he heard must have been good because after the inquiries were done the father gave Joe and his brothers his blessing to join our new venture.

Again I collected a check and a signature that gave Joe's business exclusive rights to our reservation system in the Phoenix area. The agreement was contingent on the 800 number being up and running. My assistant back in Albuquerque moved mountains and got that number set up before I left Phoenix a few days later. The time spent in Phoenix was the best time I ever had during the startup stage. I came to know Joe and his brothers very well. They were very hospitable and had numerous suggestions on how to market the system. The Phoenix brothers were to become very instrumental in helping me to build the business and even offered to give references to new prospects to the system. They realized that as the system grew so would their business because of their affiliation with the network.

A New Kind of Obstacle Course

We started to become a real national reservation system. Things felt as if they were coming together. I took off to Las Vegas, Denver, Dallas and finally Houston. At each stop I was able to locate and connect with a top notch independent operator interested in signing on with our system. I came home with more money than Terry or my father thought possible. The concept was now officially off the ground with plenty of support from the original group of reservation system participants. Now all I needed was an automated airline reservation system to complete my commitments to the participants, and to operate the business sketched out in my original blue print.

I now encountered my biggest obstacle: convincing the

major airline companies to connect my car rental reservation network to their systems. First the airlines were hard to reach. There was no one person that seemed to handle the reservation process from start to finish. Next, I had to explain to them that we were not a franchise per se. We were a collective cooperative, an affiliated group of independent car rental operators offering better service, competitive rates and quality cars for the money. I pitched our plan again and again, but everyone at the airlines I spoke with came up with some unrelated and even ill-informed excuse as to why they could not allow our company the same reservation access same service as Hertz, Avis, National, and Budget.

At this point on the obstacle course for the national reservation system I began to encounter situations that I was woefully unprepared for. I had never gone to business school. I did not know how to deal with people in big corporations and had no formal training in corporate management structure. This was a very big obstacle for me. I was ill equipped and out of my league. What I needed was help from someone with real expertise in these matters. I knew of no one. Not even my father could help.

Thus far in my business life I had overcome obstacles with hard work, gentle persuasion, chutzpa, or just old-fashioned good luck. But in this situation, the obstacle was different. I did not know or understand what I was up against and this made it an impossible to problem solve. Everything I tried fell short. None of my communication skills or strategies seemed to work. I was in water over my head. Dumbfounded with no answers, I felt isolated and incompetent.

This was a very low point for me. I lost my faith in my ability to improvise, to overcome new difficulties and succeed on the obstacle course. I had never been here before. In sports, school or business I had always found a way to land on my feet. But this time I was tripped up by what I did not know – in a world of people who spoke a different language – and I fell flat on my face. This obstacle was bigger than anything I had encountered before.

Outside of the Blue Print, Beyond Our Control

For the next few months day after day I beat my head against the wall with the big airline companies. This was my first encounter with big corporations and I found this business environment to be inefficient and frustrating. But my tenacity kept me working, kept me looking for a way in or around this obstacle. My gut instincts told me there had to be a person in one of these huge companies that would get my idea. I just couldn't seem to connect with that person.

After weeks and weeks of unproductive attempts, I made contact over the phone with a man who seemed to understand what I was trying to accomplish. He worked for the biggest airline in the business. I flew to Dallas to meet with him. He really wanted to help our business and thoroughly understood the concept of an independent rental car reservation system. We had a lot in common and hit it off on a personal and professional level.

My new contact championed my cause with the higher ups in the airline company. After a few meetings he called me in and gave me the bad news face to face: in spite of his best efforts, he could not convince his bosses to list me on their reservation system. He could not apologize enough and genuinely felt very bad about his airline's decision. I left his office dejected and depressed and returned to the airport to fly home with an empty hands and low morale. Inside and out, this kind of complete failure had not happened to me before.

Providential Shoe Shine

At the airport I had a little time before my flight home so I decided to get my shoes shined. The shoeshine man started up a conversation and asked me what kind of trip I was on. This friendly guy got an ear-full about how our startup business could not prevail with the big airline. Just before I started to tell my story to the shoe shine man a well dressed man had sat down in the chair next to me. He listened in on my sad soliloquy. After a few minutes he joined in the conversation, and asked who I was dealing with at the airline, and what did I have in mind for the business I was trying to build. After our shoes were shined this man turned to me and said he thought he could help me out.

To my shock I soon found out that this well dressed and friendly man was a top executive of the airline. He had been cruising about the airport to observe the performance of the many employees of the company. After our talk he invited me to go with him to a crude back office area where he made a telephone call to the higher ups of the airline. Within a few minutes I was on my way back to the same office where I had unsuccessfully pitched my idea a few hours before, but this time I gave my pitch to the head "Jefe" of the airline reservation system. Within a few minutes I received approval to have our company listed on the biggest airline reservation system in the world.

It seemed that Providence had intervened.

I returned to Albuquerque humbled, grateful and victorious. I had successfully assembled the network of key location car rental operators. I had our 800 number up and running, had set up a call center and now we had access to the world's largest airline reservation system.

This all happened within a few months' time. We were coming in under the projected startup budget and already producing revenues. Terry, my father and the family lawyer all contributed to the success of the system by helping me out on short notice and coming through with what was needed at each step of startup. Like me, they were very pleased and surprised that the new business was progressing so swiftly. And all of this was built upon the blue print developed in a twenty-page plan. I was ecstatic!

There were several definitive factors that enabled our success: we were following a plan that was firmly based on research and expert advice. Although I did not follow this blue print to the "T" I did constantly rely on the plan outline to guide my steps and inform my decisions. I did not wing it as I did with the car rental startup. I set goals and considered options for how I would go about executing the plan. And I set up a calendar of deadlines that incorporated a checklist of important tasks necessary for success in the new business.

When a new venture moves as fast as the national reservation system did at startup it is extremely important to be organized. Although I never went to business school, I had a college degree and was a registered nurse. Nurses have to be very organized and pay close attention to lists of details. I knew about the importance of details. What I knew about business to that point I learned from my father. Everything else I learned on the fly. This was my job training. Common sense, asking experts for advice, outlining tasks and details, calendar planning and goal setting – this combination can produce success. And let's not leave out Providential Intervention: Being in the right place at the right time and a lot of help from the guy upstairs.

Sometimes it is the things you cannot control that inhibit your success. And sometimes the things you cannot control precipitate your success. In my interactions with the national airlines I was out of my league. I did not possess the skills or have access to the resources needed to overcome the obstacles. Providence literally intervened and influenced the outcome, changed a no-win situation into an opportunity for success. You cannot plan for everything. You cannot know everything. You cannot win at everything by yourself. But you must put yourself "out there" and be available to whatever help and support, providential or otherwise, might come your way. In some situations you must let go and let God!

Don't think for a minute that you can attempt the obstacle course alone. In the previous chapter I spoke of the right people, partners and professionals that you need around you. These are all very important. And in my experience, if you think for a minute that you can successfully complete the obstacle course without God's help you are mistaken.

Planning, visualization and all the other elements I've discussed thus far are vital for a successful business enterprise. But you need faith too. In the most challenging of times, faith is the single most important component to your ultimate success.

Chapter Summary

The executive calendar identifies and defines the various tasks that have to be accomplished for business startup. This calendar can become a set of detailed outlines of and deadlines for various elements essential to operating the business. Research into the business can expand the tasks on the calendar. The calendar and outline is summarized into an executive summary and budget. These twenty pages of information are the blue print to building the new business.

However, even with good preparation and research, and a carefully organized calendar and blue print, there are components to business startup that cannot be predicted or even prepared for. At these times you have to rely on serendipity, your intuition, and your faith. Although the solution may be outside of your control, you must place yourself in a position to receive the solution that can offer alternative options that will contribute to the success of your business.

5

Knowing What You Don't Know

In spite of missteps and stumbles caused by my business naiveté, the entire experience surrounding the startup of the rental car company was a blast! Getting the reservation system up and going to this point was even more fun. But throughout the process I began to realize that chutzpa, persistence, drive and just plain luck were not enough to sustain a business long term. The obstacles thus far made it apparent that my knowledge was deficient in many areas of office operations and management, and in basic general business concepts. I needed to fill in the gaps in my knowledge.

Hitting the Books, Finding Mentors

At local bookstores I bought scores of books on business. I went to the local university book store and purchased every text on finance used in the university's business and economics classes. I scoured book catalogues and ordered titles on various topical business subjects. I wound up building a pretty impressive library. I studied the fundamentals of business and finance, and acquired a very good fiscal foundation. But after plowing through all of this helpful and worthy material I realized that book learning about the economics of business was not going to be enough. I needed mentors.

Enter Gino, my friend in the automotive business who had reminded me back when I was just getting into business to "see it like a movie." I was having trouble visualizing my next steps because I didn't know enough about those steps to even imagine them! Gino was not a college educated man but he possessed something very valuable: intelligence and experience. Once again, Gino gave me sage advice exactly when I needed it. Over lunch one day he said to me: "You cannot know everything about everything. Therefore you seek out people who know what you don't know, and surround yourself with them." It made sense.

Terry and my father were doing well with the car rental operations. The financing was in place and our new business was growing at a phenomenal pace. Life was good. However, the startup of the reservation system was a whole new ball game: I needed to have a thorough understanding of and working knowledge about communication technology, finance, and corporate management, and also understand the dynamics of the travel industry. I needed to absorb this information quickly. So, taking Gino's advice to surround myself with people who knew what I did not, I began hiring individuals who had experience and expertise in those areas of business that I was frankly ignorant about. These people brought with them a wide spectrum of skills and were proficient in various aspects and elements of the business I was trying to build – from the burgeoning personal computer business to the world of travel agents. Their job was to teach and guide. My job was to listen and learn.

My father and Terry started to see a lot of strangers around the office and questioned why this or that person was important and why they were getting so much of my time? Simple: I was short on the knowledge needed to make smart, informed decisions about the reservation business. What might look to be a lot of money thrown into thin air was actually just the opposite: this was money well spent as it was building a base of information that would allow me to move forward with the new business. It felt right: I was paying tuition for an internship in my own business.

The services of many of these experts and mentors were only needed for a short period of time. There was a lot of turnover around our office, people coming and going, new hires in, temporary hires departing, consultants and professionals whirling about. Although this is not a situation I would recommend for everyone's business, this ad hoc method of information gathering and company building was very effective for my business education.

Through this in-office mentoring process I absorbed mountains of information. It was alternately overwhelming and exhausting, exhilarating and energizing. At the very least, I was gaining a very clear understanding of just how much I did not know! That was the key to utilizing this kind of crash course internship: understanding what I lacked and then taking direction from people who could fill in the gaps. After a year of this in-office education I began to assemble in my mind's eye the complete picture of what was needed to put together what was turning out to be a monster of a new business. In the beginning I did not realize just how big the national car rental reservation business would turn out to be.

The Good, the Bad & the Opportunists

Inviting a lot of experts who were also strangers into the business, even for short periods of time, brought with it a certain element of risk. There were some people along the way that just wanted to ride my wave, to take what they could and vanish. There were others who wanted to exploit our venture, individuals who had no other interest but to take advantage of the opportunity that was being created by my father, Terry and myself. And some of those "experts" were people that claimed to know a lot about certain things or to have experience in a particular field, but who, in fact, knew very little or nothing at all. All of these undesirables were quickly jettisoned from the business.

Unfortunately, discovering the true nature of these

charlatans and then ridding a business of these parasites does not always bring an end to the unwanted entanglement. A disgruntled ex-employee can use rumor and gossip to skew the facts surrounding their dismissal from a company, and unflattering untruths can hit the street pretty quickly. In our case, following the firing of several "bad hires" at our company, their attempts to smear our venture were thwarted by friends in the business community who knew our operations and defended our professionalism. But even if the rumor mill is quickly closed down, this sort of personal and professional harassment is stressful and energy sapping.

This part of the obstacle course is not easily prepared for. The best preparation and defense is what was discussed in chapter 3: when selecting partners, associates and employees take time to know who you are dealing with. Don't be hasty when bringing someone into the business, even short term. Define boundaries and expectations, and have a formal agreement that specifically delineates the roles and terms of the professional relationship. The best professionals will prefer having boundaries and defined roles. The scoundrels will be threatened by your insistence on specifics and expectations. Perhaps their real intentions will surface before your business becomes entwined with them.

Be very careful about whom you add to your team. Some of the wannabe's can fool you and waste valuable time, money and personal energy. I've had my share of scoundrels.

Staying Connected to the Gut Instinct

Team building takes time and effort. The old saying "You must kiss a lot of frogs…" is very true. Like at the startup of a new venture, this part of the business obstacle course – finding a strong team – calls on our intuition and our people skills. Hopefully, after overcoming the challenges thus far we have begun to develop a sense about people. By now the inner voice is a continuous source of guidance as we evaluate individuals and what they may or may not bring to the work place. Our intuition helps us choose people who will add value to our team.

Hindsight is twenty-twenty, and sometimes that's the only way we come to clearly see our mistakes and learn from them. Case in point: John. John was a friend of Terry's who was involved in real estate. Upon learning about our new car rental business John came to us and said that he had experience taking a company public. John said he could raise private capital and could help us with the next phase of the business development. We invited John to join our office. After several months on the team, nothing John had said he was going to do had in fact taken place. John's ineptitude and empty promises caused the business to squander several opportunities. It also cost the business time and money.

John's misrepresentation of his skills and experience, and our inability to recognize John's deceptions, sent us down a very expensive and time consuming path that ultimately went nowhere the business needed or wanted to go. The lesson? Sometimes because we are acquainted with an individual we skip formalities and don't examine what professional experience they are actually bringing to the business. Familiarity with a person does not mean you know how competent they are professionally, and it certainly doesn't mean you should trust them with your business' future. Check out everyone who might be involved in your operations.

The saga with John did not end when he was terminated. He attempted to sue us for what he thought was due him. The law suit went nowhere but more time and money was wasted. The value of people is in the choosing. Finding the right person for the job is not easy. Personnel selection takes time to learn and requires skills that combine proficient personnel management and the good old gut instinct. Becoming adept at early detection of the holes, half truths and exaggerations in someone's resume takes practice. People skills are learned through trial and error, and from time to time you may select the wrong person. Catalogue the experience; take it as a lesson not to be repeated again.

Good Guys

We were six months into the development of the reservation business when Gino re-emerged in my life and was again of real help to me and the business. Over several casual meetings on a host of subjects I felt I needed his counsel on, Gino reminded me, once again, about visualization, and encouraged me to continue using this process of the active imagination with my business concerns and goals. He also gave me concrete help and directed me to people and contacts that could help me purchase the kind of vehicles we needed.

In the wake of our disastrous situation with John, Gino reminded me that an entrepreneur cannot be all things to all situations. He suggested I surround myself with people who are smarter than me. It finally dawned on me that Gino was exactly the sort of person he was talking about! Gino was a cut above everyone else because he had no ulterior motives: Gino never expected a thing in return for his advice and counsel. It was reward enough for Gino to help a kid who needed a little guidance with his first business. This is the kind of advisor one needs: someone who is objective, intelligent, experienced, thoughtful and generous. This is what makes a successful person and a successful businessman! Pass it along.

Over the next year, throughout the process of building the reservation system, I often thought of Gino and what he would do in a particular situation. Although his lessons were simple they have stuck with me to this day. When I seek the advice of others I look to see what their motivations are, or if they have an agenda or ulterior motive that is not good for the business. I compare advisors to Gino, and always look for the qualities of intelligence, experience and bigheartedness. Gino was one of the good guys.

Chance Meetings

There were many good guys who assisted me while I was building the business. Although the difficult people tend to stand out, they are finally overshadowed by the genuinely helpful people who emerged as associates and partners. Ken was an important mentor I met by chance, a man who was genuinely interested in assisting our business. A marketing professor at the local university, Ken called me on the telephone after reading an article in the local newspaper about me and the company. He had the chutzpa to pick up the phone and give me a call just to talk about the article and what I was doing. It was a long conversation. He seemed like a real gentleman over the telephone so I set up a meeting to visit with him in person.

From the minute I met Ken we hit it off. Ken was straightforward and to the point. During that first meeting he told me he wanted to "hitch to my star." And Ken was the kind of person I wanted hitched to my star, if I indeed had one! I needed a guy like Ken and having him along for the ride meant the ride was going to be safer, smoother and have a better chance at succeeding. Ken was smart, experienced and had a solid understanding of what we were attempting to do. Ken had sound credentials and was well known at the time throughout the local university circles. He had done consulting and others have had very favorable experiences with him. This time I did a little background check of my own and Ken was checking out very well.

At a young age Ken had started his own successful business in Canada. He knew exactly what I was going through. From those first conversations it was obvious what he knew and what he had experienced. Ken was someone who knew a lot more than I did, and he shared his knowledge immediately.

No hidden agenda. Within a very short time after that first meeting we started working together. Ken frequently stopped by the office and I would catch him up on matters concerning the reservation operations. These meetings were nothing more than casual conversations but they were very informative and Ken became a valuable mentor.

Ken became a director on the board of the new reservation system corporation. His expertise, professionalism and marketing experience were obvious to everyone on the board, and Ken quickly gained the respect of both my father and Terry. Ken was a busy person, and he kept his visits to the office brief. Ken also mentored me by phone. His counsel and advice was always on target and useful to the business. Ken's contributions were about high quality not huge quantity.

Ken taught me the basics of marketing. The development and uses of technology were important to the business' growth, but we were also becoming a company whose main focus would have to be cutting edge marketing. Remember the providential shoeshine that introduced me to the man who opened the door to the national reservation system? It was equally providential that Ken read the newspaper article and then decided to telephone me because Ken's expertise in marketing (remember he was a marketing professor) was exactly what the business needed: I didn't know it yet, but I needed someone to mentor me and the business through the world of marketing. And that someone found me.

Building an Orchestra: Capital Formation

It was becoming evident to me, and to my partners, board of directors and advisors that the business needed more talented people. I was still functioning like a one man band. I needed an orchestra of people to build this operation into a nationally positioned company. We began hiring more "musicians" for the orchestra but we needed more capital if we were going to make bigger and better music. So, once again I found myself plunging ahead into something I knew nothing about: capital formation, which is raising money from private individuals to infuse into your company. I asked Ken's advice at this juncture, and also went to see my first banker, Ben. Ben and I had remained friends and colleagues even though I did not bank with his institution anymore. I simply asked Ben if he would help me understand corporate financing. Ben was happy to help.

In a few short weeks Ben gave me the equivalent of a graduate course in corporate finance. Ben moved through this course very quickly. I had to sit up, pay attention, and soak up every word Ben spoke because it was all relevant. Ben taught me how to begin to go about raising money. Ken's expertise was not in corporate finance but he was able help me with the financial bottom line, and to fill in the gaps on the type and size of budget needed to grow the business into a marketing company. Ken was really in his element and on his best game. This was a team effort.

This was a good time for me and I knew it. I was being tutored by two smart men. I was learning new things about business and finance every day, preparing to raise needed capital and bring in more personnel to our company. I could visualize the orchestra and hear the music the business would soon be making. The reservation venture was moving forward and measurable progress was being made almost every single day. It was again an exciting time.

During this time I decided that I needed to focus most if not all of my energy on raising capital. I did not know that this could be detrimental. In the business world scores of entrepreneurs attempt to be all things to all situations within their business. And most of the time, we manage to multi-task well enough to keep the business moving forward. However, I was about to learn that capital formation is an all consuming task. Capital formation cannot be done part time. It becomes your full time job. Everything else at the office is pushed aside.

In retrospect, I should have looked harder outside the office for the right person to tackle capital formation for our company. At the time I believed I was the only obvious choice. Terry and my father were busy with the car rental business, and my father was overseeing the title business as well. Because I had put together the money for the rental car company, and now had Ben and Ken tutoring me, I assumed that I could easily undertake capital formation. I decided I was the logical person for this job. Unfortunately I was ignoring another teacher, Gino, and his advice to hire in people to do those jobs I knew nothing about. I was about to encounter an obstacle even larger and more challenging than those of the past. But being ignorant of my ignorance, I pushed full speed ahead.

At this juncture in the obstacle course, following the advice Gino gave me would have served all of us in the business very well. Instead, I decided that Ben and Ken had given me enough information, and that I was now sufficiently knowledgeable about capital formation to raise the needed money. How hard could this be? What obstacles could possibly get in the way of me raising a few hundred thousand dollars, or maybe even a few million? I could not have been more brainless and cavalier. I should have been asking the experts about possible obstacles! Capital formation was not going to be an easy process. My mistakes detailed in the upcoming chapters will serve as examples of what not to do!

Going Public

It was clear that we were going to need a few million dollars to continue to build the business. I discussed this with Ben who explained that I was going to have to take the company public. Going public? What was that? Ben took me through the steps that would be involved with this process: First we had to raise a small amount of private money from friends and family and former enemies, as they say, to assist in covering the expenses associated with going public. Then we would need to hire accountants and lawyers to file a registration statement or offering circular with the Securities Exchange Commission (SEC) after we had located and retained an underwriter to sell the stock being offered.

My dad and I had done well with small cap stocks during the penny stock boom of the early eighties. So this is how they did it?! Going public! Ben's opinion was that I could successfully take on this task. Therefore I thought I could do it, too. I approached my father and Terry and convinced them, and soon everybody around me believed I could raise the capital we needed. This was going to be the challenge of my life.

Armed with Ben's 101 course on corporate finance and going public, I set off to formulate yet another new business plan. From Ken I had gathered a mountain of information about the kind and size of budget necessary to take the reservation system to the next level. From various associates and experts within and outside of the company I had catalogued enormous amounts of information on how to assemble the infrastructure of the operation. I was bursting at the seams with useful information and felt thoroughly prepared to take on capital formation. What could possibly go wrong? This mammoth file of information would only mitigate my risk. Right? Wrong! There was so much more that I did not know! If someone had told me I was a fish out of water I might have noticed that I was miles away from any river.

Remember how important it is to know what you don't know? I did not know what I did not know and so did not have a clue about what I was missing.

With Ben's help I began to put together a very crude corporate finance plan. Today, when I put finance plans together for my clients, I often think back about that very first plan! It was a pretty sorry document. Because I did not know what I did not know I thought it was a work of art.

The plan began with the raising of the private capital that would provide working capital and fund the expenses of going public. The plan also included borrowing money from a commercial bank to fund daily operations and provide additional working capital. This financial blueprint had a list of the people I thought I could raise money from – some 150 in all. It named the bank that we were already dealing with as the primary lender because our relationship with that bank was in good shape. It was a simple plan, and although this was about raising money, was really no different from other business plans I had put together. It looked good to me.

When I think back on this particular time in my business life I just shake my head: I had no idea how close I was to total financial incineration. To my inexperienced eyes, everything seemed to fit. My decision to be the person in charge of capital formation seemed grounded in solid reasoning: I had gathered a lot of expert information and had really good advisors around me. It all made sense.

Specialists: Why We Need Them & Why We Must Become One

It cannot be said enough: it is critically important to the success of your business that you understand at the outset that you cannot and will not know everything necessary to run your business. Period. Accept your limitations at the start and every day thereafter.

Hiring capable people and recruiting good advisors is vital to the success of your burgeoning business. Just as doctors specialize in a certain area of medicine, so do professionals in banking, finance, bookkeeping, marketing and public relations specialize within their fields. There is a good reason for this: no one can know and do everything, and so professionals specialize in a particular field. We must become specialists, too, and accept that we may be proficient, even an expert, in one or two arenas of our business, but that in other arenas, we need to bring in a specialist. When we encounter an obstacle that demands expertise beyond our own knowledge base, we must recognize our lack and hire the best people we can find.

Even though we have researched and gathered information from multiple sources and learned a good deal about say capital formation, this information only makes us better able to make intelligent, informed decisions as we seek out the right people to help our business take on this new obstacle. Becoming educated about the nuts and bolts of a particular arena in business does not make us instant experts. It just gives us a good foundation in that field of study. We ask better questions perhaps. Just like they say on some television programs – "Don't attempt this stunt at home..." – some tasks in business are best left to the professionals who are specialists in that task. In fact, in the long run a specialist will cost you less and save you time.

As I have become older I have come to value my time

and energy, and have learned to prioritize how my time and energy are used. In my twenties I believed I had an inexhaustible source of time and energy. Time passed and it took with it a lot of my energy! I began to realize I am exhaustible and vulnerable. I also began to realize that time and energy in the business world are about productivity. And productivity or lack thereof directly impacts a business' financial stability. Any action or decision that increases my own productivity – saves me valuable time and energy – increases the business' productivity. Hiring in the expertise the business needs is absolutely the best choice, always!

I have made my official entrance into my fifties and realize there are only so many productive hours in the day. Those productive hours are best utilized doing those tasks I am proficient in. I have learned to seek out help before attempting to overcome an obstacle I know little or nothing about. There is no need to re-invent the wheel: better to consult those who have already successfully overcome the obstacle. Perhaps the wisdom of age is about knowing when we need assistance and then putting the ego aside and gladly asking for and accepting a helping hand.

Chapter Summary:

The more we learn the more we understand what we do not know. And as we learn how much we do not know, we also learn how to find and ask for help. The goal in business is to overcome obstacles using good sense, good judgment and our accumulated experience as we move along the course. To save our own time and energy we hire in the expert when we recognize that our knowledge base is not enough. We understand that sometimes getting through a section of the obstacle course involves a team effort. Paying for that team support is a good use of our resources. Knowing what we don't know is a skill that serves both the individual and the business.

6

Banking, Finance and Mom's Money

My first lesson in banking was one that I would never forget: Always do business with a bank large enough to meet your needs. By this time in the business startup I thought that obstacle was well behind me, but I still had more to learn about the world of banking. There were outside forces coming at us that would make my life a living hell and force me to face obstacles I never even knew existed. These same outside influences would almost bring me, my father and Terry to total financial ruin.

As mentioned before, I had formulated a new plan that included borrowing more money from my bank and also raising private capital. This plan would demand all of my

attention for an indefinite period of time as you will learn
in this chapter. I did not know how difficult this part of the
obstacle course was going to be: even though Ben had taught
me about the mechanics of fundraising, he did not prepare
me for how difficult a task it was going to be to raise private
capital.

The first step of the new plan called for me to borrow money
from the bank I was currently doing business with. I went
to discuss the need for a new loan with my banker who
listened intently while I pitched the reservation system to
him. He was surprised that a local small business that he
had been financing was about to launch a very ambitious
plan that would give this little company a national presence.
I explained that I needed to borrow money to assist in
the financing of the basic operations. We needed money
for hardware, and to hire personnel for the reservation
operation.

The banker's response was, well, a tad veiled. He said he
thought the plan was fantastic but still needed to take it to
the loan committee. The odd thing about this was that his
loan limit as a bank officer was the same as the bank's loan
limit. He never needed approval from the loan committee.
He patted me on the back and told me not to worry because
everything was going to be alright. I left not knowing the
real story.

Friends, Family and Former Enemies

I began to talk to individuals about investing in my company. I had prepared a list and met with them one by one. First up was my father-in-law. I set up a lunch meeting and shared with him how the company was going to be expanded. He was surprised: he had no idea that we had any sort of dream to expand the company. He said that it seemed that it was just yesterday that I opened the car rental operation. Being the ever supportive father-in-law, he invested. Furthermore, he said he would help raise a few more dollars for me. He suggested that I speak with his brother-in-law, Dave, so he could invest. Dave invested as well. Then Dave turned me on to a few investors and so it went. Both Dave and my father-in-law were a great help. They were very supportive and to this day I'm grateful for the way they gave me such a positive start to a very difficult task.

This initial stage of fund raising all seemed to run very smoothly. Close family and friends had a lot of confidence in the entire plan. They had seen what we had done with the rental car venture and were impressed with our progress and ideas for expansion of the business. I was following the advice of the experts and building an investment group from within the company's circle of friends, family and "former enemies." All the best books about corporate finance tell you that this is the best way to begin the process. Maybe something I read along the way had sunk in. And maybe luck was involved a bit, too.

Throughout this time the title and registration company my father and I owned continued to make investments into the reservation system: cash advances, loans, buying stock in the company, leasing equipment, just about everything you can imagine. Our other business was very profitable and had tremendous cash flow. We all believed in the new venture so why not continue to support the reservation system? The reservation system had a mountain of potential.

Overloaded and Underfunded

During the capital raising process I did not dedicate a lot of my time to the day to day operations, or to seeking out and selling more territories. I was consumed with raising money and getting the company public. My time was filled with meetings and conversations with potential investors, and following up on referrals from new shareholders. I was also coordinating the advertising for the reservation system. I learned that coordinating all the aspects of a business' advertising was an overwhelming job. I had no background or education in the arts of advertising. I should have known by now to stick to the things I do best. The entire advertising process was a new field to me. Where were the experts?! Sometimes you can only learn by doing. Again, I had to learn the hard way.

All of a sudden, almost overnight, my capital raising activities came to a sudden halt. The upswing stalled and the money stopped flowing. Everyone I spoke with about investing turned me down. I hit a brick wall. I had secured over a hundred and fifty thousand dollars, but that seemed to be all the capital I could raise. I became desperate and started talking to total strangers referred to me by people who had turned me down! I didn't see at the time how these referrals were nothing more than empty suggestions meant to momentarily appease me and get me out the door. For weeks I went from one "no" to another. Terry could not even persuade his closest of friends to invest. And my father had little or no luck with his close associates and friends.

I finally ran out of names and referrals. I remember one night I was home thinking again about who I could talk to about investing. The news came on television. The newscaster went to my church, and I decided I would give him a try. That is how desperate I was. But even after friends arranged a meeting with him, and I gave him my best pitch, I received only his firm NO!

I understand now how my little city was a small town where there were not many people with the kind of money I was looking for. And actually raising that initial one hundred fifty thousand was not bad for my first time out. My town, like most, was also controlled by the "old boys club." These guys were the big wigs in town and when it came to a business going public they dictated if a little guy could even get in the game. I was not well received by these guys. They thought I was a young dumb punk. They were not too far off. As a result they would have nothing to do with my project. Several of them put the word out on the street that our business was a flash in the pan.

Local politics are important and impact local businesses.

You must learn who the players are and how to interact with them. Had I catered a little more to this group and gotten to know them better, capitalization might have gone easier. Politics are always a part of the equation in building a business.

Needless to say, the capitalization activities and challenges overwhelmed my time and energy. I had absolutely nothing left for the business' advertising needs and so hired an advertising firm to assist with the placement of magazine ads. We also needed a graphic artist to design the ads we were placing.

It seems that difficulties on the obstacle course are never spaced out in manageable challenges, but come all at once. Just as the money raising campaign came to a halt so did the level of trust with the advertising firm. Remember what I said earlier about hiring people you can trust? Well this little debacle with the ad agency is just a prime example of why this axiom is so important.

The advertising firm we hired was paid on a commission from actual ad sales, and was also paid a fee for the professional time needed to design and develop the ads. The ad agency placed ads without approval from me or anyone else at the office. The result was they obligated us to tens of thousands of dollars of advertising bills we had no idea existed. All of the sudden bills were showing up at the office for ads placed in major magazines advertising the eight hundred reservation number. Mind you these ads were generating higher than normal reservations but the cost was astronomical. When I approached the ad company they assured me that I had approved the expensive ads. No proof of any kind could be produced by their office verifying their claim that I had given them the go ahead. I fired them immediately.

Although we had been taken advantage of and could legally go after the ad company, my father said that we needed to preserve our reputation. We had received some measurable benefits from the deal and we needed to do the right thing. And suing the company was not going to be worth the effort in the long run. I told my dad that we had a host of other commitments and did not have enough money in our account to pay these new and unanticipated advertising bills. My dad listened to my fears and grievances and then said that I needed to speak with my mother and right away. I left the meeting puzzled that he thought I needed a talk with my mom.

Mother: Teacher and Banker

I called my mother and explained to her the situation around the office. She said I needed to come over and talk more about the problem. So I drove to the house and told her the entire story of how the ad agency had thrown us under the bus so they could generate commissions, and how I had run out of steam on the money raising front. After she heard the whole sad story of my business misadventures my mother went upstairs and pulled out a shoebox full of US Savings Bonds. She handed this box of bonds to me and explained that she would lend me the money. She said I would need to pay her back, but for now I needed to pay these people off, put this hiccup behind me, pull myself up by the boot straps and move forward.

I drove my mother to the bank where she cashed $40,000 worth of bonds (back in the day when you could do such a thing), handed me a cashier's check for the entire amount and told me to get back to work. I was stunned, relieved and burdened at the same time. I was stunned because I had no idea that my mother had saved so diligently over the years and believe me I did not make a dent in the shoebox. She told me that this was rainy day money she had put away over many years working for a major retailer. This was her "safe money." One third of every paycheck went for bonds and to buy stock in the company she worked for. My mother said this was that rainy day the money had been put away for, and it needed to be used wisely. I was relieved that I had the money to live up to our business obligations and take care of what could have ballooned into a major hassle and headache. And I felt burdened with the responsibility to pay back my mother, and also burdened by the sudden realization that I had a big responsibility to all of our shareholders. The weight of the entire situation landed on me like a ton of bricks.

This precise series of events needed to happen: I needed to wake up and realize my responsibility to our shareholders. When you raise money and sell stock in your company you in essence take on partners. You have a duty to these partners to live up to your business commitments because everything you do impacts their investment. You also have a responsibility to protect the shareholders and the company from harm. Since that time of my wakeup call I have worked from the premise that you protect and take care of your partners first, and your partners will protect and take care of you. The situation with the ad agency brought this truth home. I began to think very differently about what I was doing as an entrepreneur, and how my choices and actions affected the business and the people involved with the business. I became less focused on an individual task and instead focused on my responsibilities to the whole operation.

This would not be the only time my mother would come to the rescue. She knew what she was doing when she handed me the cash from her bonds. She had raised me to be a responsible person and was confident that all she had taught me about commitment and honesty would steer me through this crisis. Perhaps the most important rule my mother taught me was to honor a promise. Honor commitments. And that's exactly what I was doing: honoring my commitments to the magazines that had run the ads, to the stockholders, and ultimately, when I paid her back, honoring my promise to her. This was my mother's teachings transformed into action. She was very astute.

I paid the magazines companies off and had a few extra dollars to continue to fund the operations. My mother was the boost I needed, and bailed me out of what could have been a very bad situation. She remains my number one supporter and banker to this day.

Getting to the Truth of the Matter

A month passed and I finally heard back from my banker. He said that the loan committee thought my new venture and the capital needed to underwrite it was too much of a risk for them to consider. They were not going to make the loan. After that phone call we all felt pretty dejected around the office. Maybe our plan was too ambitious?

It took a few weeks for us to learn through the community grapevine that our inability to secure a loan had nothing to do with our business or plan. The bank was in serious trouble with the regulators and had just received their Cease and Desist Order from the Comptroller of the Currency. The bank officer was simply blowing a smokescreen when he told me his loan committee wouldn't loan our business any money. That bank couldn't loan anyone any money!

The bank never contacted us about their situation. I heard about their regulatory difficulties serendipitously from a friend. The bank's condition and their inability to loan us money soon began to affect our rental car company. We could no longer buy more cars to meet the growing demands. Our fleet growth began to stagger and business began to flatten off at a time we could have realized significant growth. A bank that could not lend money was the farthest thing from my mind. At the time, I did not even realize that banks could be prevented from lending by the government. But until I accidentally learned about the bank's regulatory issues, I believed our floundering business and declined loan application was all my fault.

Upon learning this shocking bit of information about the bank I set up a meeting with my banker and confronted him on the issue. He did come clean and admitted that the loan committee had nothing to do with our loan being turned down. He maintained, however, that the regulatory problems were only temporary and things at the bank would return to normal very soon. He promised that once the dust settled with the Comptroller the bank would make the loan for our new reservation system, and also lend more money for the fleet we needed to expand our rental business. This should have been good news, but I left feeling very uncomfortable. I could not quite put my finger on the gut feeling I was getting but that banker seemed inexplicably nervous.

I met with my father and Terry and gave them the lowdown about the bank's condition and how it had affected our loan request. My father was shocked. Terry was stunned. At the end of the meeting we agreed that we needed to find a new bank as soon as possible because this bank's troubles were now affecting our business. I was elected to hunt around town and see what bank might help us.

Guilty by Association

The main reason that our bank was in trouble was that they had engaged in a lot of very risky oil and gas, and commercial real estate loans. Of course, every bank in the community knew about this bank's risky ventures. As a result if you were a customer of the bank it was automatically assumed by other banks that you were a bad loan risk. Thus, because our business had taken a loan from the troubled bank, our loan request was turned down by every bank in the community.

Other bank's loan officers never even looked at our financial statements. We just had to be a risky loan because we had borrowed money from the bank now in trouble with the regulators. We were making money and our cash flow was positive. We made our loan payments on time. To an impartial judge, we were actually a good loan risk. But in the small town banking and business community, we were guilty by association.

Other companies and businesses in the community that were clients of the bad bank were experiencing the same thing. Many good businesses were just assumed to be bad loan risks and thus not given a fair loan assessment by other banks. A few weeks after my meeting with my banker the word finally hit the streets that the bad bank was going to fail. There was a mad rush by businesses to find new banking relationships. We all found that many of the local bank doors were closed to our loan applications. You could open a checking account but the window was closed for borrowing. Many good and decent businesses suffered.

Over the past year my father, never one to be caught flat footed, had been quietly cultivating a relationship with a small bank in town. Lorraine, the banker he had become acquainted with, became a long term friend and advisor to our business. Her bank could not meet all of our needs but Lorraine was a generous and creative problem solver, and

suggested that a few small signature notes along with some
personal loans would at least bridge the company's needs
at the time. But we still could not obtain the loan to buy
a new fleet of cars, and the car rental business was really
beginning to suffer and stall.

Soon our bank failed. Through a series of very complicated
events involving the bank's takeover and the purchase
of its assets our business, like many others, was left to
deal with the RTC (Resolution Trust Corporation), the
government entity set up to deal with the failure of various
types of banking institutions. What a mess. The RTC was
little more than a bunch of bureaucrats with little or no
banking experience. They had even less experience dealing
with private companies, and no idea what pressures and
difficulties a business caught up in the quagmire of a failed
bank was going through. These people were clueless as to
the nature of their job, and had no empathy for the dazed
and confused business people who through no fault of their
own found themselves seated across the desk from them. For
months, we and dozens of other businesses were bounced
around from agent to agent. What a disaster. I could not
have imagined this obstacle in my wildest of dreams.

We were in a full blown crisis: we could not raise any more
private money for the reservation system. We could not
borrow a dime from any bank in town because we were
tainted and scarred by the nasty shrapnel created by the bad
bank. And we ourselves were now under investigation by
RTC. Could it get any worse?

Two Steps Forward, Three Steps Back: Con Artists and Charlatans

In spite of all these difficulties, I was still out trying to raise private capital. Ben was introducing me to investment bankers that were interested in taking the company public. I was meeting these guys under very informal circumstances. Lunches and cocktails seemed to be the way Ben wanted me to get the feel of talking to and interacting with this bunch. There were no formal office meetings up to this point. This was my training ground.

Now mind you mine was not a sexy high tech business. Many of the new companies of the day going public were high tech. Mine was not among them. I was just offering a good meat and potatoes business with a lot of potential.

My first formal office meeting set up by Ben was in Denver with Jack, CEO of a small penny stock investment banking house. This was essentially my first formal pitch. To my surprise Jack got it. He liked simple businesses with good growth potential. Soon after the meeting we received our first Letter of Intent from Jack's investment banking firm. I began to get re-energized. I thought maybe after hundreds of "no's" I was headed in the right direction after all. My father and Terry were thrilled. We believed we were again on our way.

The word hit the street that we had a Letter of Intent. Soon every charlatan in town was at our door step wanting to jump on board and take us for a ride. After a while we were persuaded by a few of these parasites that we should get this man Sandy involved in the deal and have him take us public. Sandy was a lawyer and a promoter. Everybody was saying Sandy is the only one who can get you public. Everyone but Ben. Ben was discouraging me, my father and Terry to do any business with Sandy. Ben knew all about Sandy and he kept saying this was one really bad guy.

But Sandy had several high profile public companies to his credit. Some of these companies were high fliers. Naturally, we were impressed. Everyone knew who Sandy was when it came to going public in the small cap markets. He seemed to be the go-to player. Over and over we kept hearing the same thing: cancel your agreement with Jack and get Sandy to handle your deal.

It is here that we committed a grievous mistake and took the advice of charlatans who in fact had nothing invested in our venture. They were like bees buzzing around us with nothing but bad pollen to put in our flower. To our detriment we listened to their advice and took their "counsel."

Jack could have successfully syndicated the public offering. He had a genuine interest in the company and the transaction as a whole. But we were being told by the charlatans that Jack was a small time player, and that he was not going to last. Sandy, Sandy, Sandy was all we were hearing. Sandy was the only real player.

Hence we met with Sandy. Enter Sandy, this creepy, arrogant, pompous, cocky stock promoter. I should have known better, should have listened to my gut instinct about this guy, but the bees buzzing about were drowning out my inner voice and numbing my intuition. During our first meeting with Sandy I got a really bad uneasy feeling. But I ignored it. Sandy guaranteed he would get an underwriter of significant stature and standing for us that would insure the public offering would be successfully completed. It didn't feel right but it sounded good.

In addition, Sandy said he wanted to make an investment in the company. This was his way of demonstrating he was part of the team. Sandy asked the price of the private stock I was selling. I told him. Sandy then offered ten percent of that figure, explaining that he deserved this discount because he was going to make us rich. He did go on to say that if we needed anything, including raising the money for the expenses of the public offering he would be there to help. In the back ground the bees were chiming in with agreement. Sandy wound up paying two thousand dollars for about ten percent of the company. What a bargain for him. What a mistake for us.

A few days later we cancelled the deal with Jack. He was very disappointed. I was honest with Jack and shared with him what we were being told – that this guy Sandy, because of who he was, guaranteed he would get the deal done. Jack knew who Sandy was. Jack tried his best in a gentlemanly way to persuade us not to go with Sandy. Jack said Sandy was not long for the world of corporate finance because some of the things he was doing were not kosher. Even after this conversation with Jack we went ahead with our cancellation of the Letter of Intent.

About this same time Sandy set up a meeting with a new investment banker, Ronnie. Unbeknownst to us Ronnie and Sandy had pre-cut a deal. Ronnie had been assured by Sandy that the offering would be completely syndicated with his own group. Ronnie would just sit back and enjoy the ride. Unknown to Ronnie was that Sandy would use fictitious names and accounts of people that did not exist, as Sandy had done in public offerings past.

In the meeting with Ronnie, I did my best to put on a first class pitch. I did not know that Ronnie would have issued a Letter of Intent no matter what I said or what I was pitching. For all he cared I could have been mowing lawns. At the meeting Ronnie said I would be receiving a Letter of Intent within a few days. He also mentioned I would use a specific law firm to represent me. I was told that same thing by Sandy: this was standard operating procedure.

As promised, here came the Letter of Intent. As promised I hired the law firm as instructed. And away we went. At this point we needed to fund the massive expenses of the public offering. I had raised some money but these funds were earmarked for marketing and operations. I went back to Sandy and asked for his aforementioned and promised help. He looked at me like I was an idiot. Red faced and angry, Sandy said raising the funds for the public offering was my responsibility. If he was going to raise private money he would just do the entire deal himself; we would not get anything. I told Sandy that I thought he was part of the team; I reminded him that he had said if we needed help with anything he'd be there. Sandy ended the conversation and told me to leave; he did not have time to waste on this ridiculous subject. Wow! I was shocked. I did not know what to think or what to do.

I told my father about the encounter. He was furious. It was clear to him that this relationship was not going to work. He called Sandy and set up a meeting. At this meeting with my father Sandy suddenly became a different person: he was gentlemanly, cordial and polite. My father was very firm with Sandy and reminded him of his commitment. Even so, even my father got nowhere on the subject of Sandy helping us raise private capital.

The bottom line was that Sandy wanted more ownership. Sandy wanted the rest of us to have a minority interest in our own company. After that meeting my father said to Terry and me that we should seriously consider getting out of this deal. As I said earlier my father placed enormous value on making and keeping your commitments. Obviously Sandy did not and this did not sit well with my father.

We had a commitment from a bona fide underwriter. We cancelled it because we were swayed by all the little bees buzzing about. We should have stuck to building a relationship with the first underwriter Jack. This was new territory for us and we just did not know any better. Now we were stuck with this creep who obviously was setting us up for something that we were all sure was not good.

All the while John, the guy I mentioned previously, was in the background telling us he had a lot of connections, urging us to get away from Sandy and let him put the deal together. Well we could not go back to Jack and going forward with Sandy was not for us so we decided that we needed to get out and move forward with John.

My father, Terry and I had a meeting with Sandy. Sandy re-iterated his claim that he had never made any commitment to raise private capital for our public offering. In fact, all three of us had heard Sandy make this commitment. At this meeting Sandy again said if we gave him more stock he would consider raising funds. Sandy then told us if we wanted him out of the way we could pay him twenty-five thousand dollars for the stock he already owned. If we failed to comply with his demands he would tie us up in court for years and we would never get public.

What a sleaze bag! We left the meeting and privately considered our options. After much discussion we decided to take Sandy out even though it meant spending cash we needed for the operations of the business.

As soon as we took Sandy out of the company the Letter of Intent with Ronnie went south as we expected. So we went forward with John. Unfortunately, John wound up being a total flop. Nothing he claimed he could do for us materialized. None of his contacts were real. John wound up wasting almost six months of our time and tens of thousands of dollars. After the debacle with John I really believed our public offering was dead.

A Lesson Learned

Looking back over our experience thus far and reviewing our decisions brought to light one very sobering fact: we had been put through the ringer largely because of our own ignorance. We had first selected a good sound underwriter, Jack, and things had looked pretty good. Jack was interested in and really understood our business, and he genuinely believed in our potential. But instead of listening to Jack we began to listen to people who had no vested interest in our endeavor, people who just wanted to play armchair quarterback and take our profits out from under us. Against our better judgment and gut instinct we went with an "expert" who we were warned was a really bad guy to be involved with. In retrospect it seems obvious that we chose Sandy out of naiveté, inexperience and even greed. Perhaps we chose him because he represented an easy way out. Or in. Maybe we chose Sandy because we felt powerless, small, and desperate. Which we were. In any case our decision process was flawed. We were responsible for the mistake. This was to be a critical stage in our development as a business and we needed to find and build the team of people who had the company and our best interests at heart.

As stated earlier it is critical that you chose people to work with you whom you trust. You must build a team whose common interest and stated purpose is the company's future and long term well being. Choose people who add value to the company. As the misadventures with Sandy and John, and with our bank, taught our company it is imperative to work with individuals, vendors and banking institutions that have earned and maintained solid community standing and widely respected reputations. The advertising company met none of these criteria. In the case of the bank we first worked with, we did not know how to investigate the fiscal health and loan capacity of a bank. In the case of Sandy, well, we ignored our gut instincts and learned the hard way that there are no short cuts to a public offering.

All of these events happened over a very short period of time – a little over six months. Taking a company public should take time but our case things moved very rapidly. Too rapidly. So fast that we did not have or take the time to review our choices, ask questions, think and rethink decisions. We allowed events to control us. We should have been controlling these events. Instead, we climbed onto a roller coaster that was out of control with no brakes.

Chapter Summary

It cannot be said enough: do everything in your power to influence events and to maintain control over each step your business takes towards a public offering. Most of all allow plenty of time to think through challenges and access possible shortfalls. Take the time to evaluate people. And remember there are no real shortcuts to achieving your goals

In retrospect the period during which we pursued the public offering had not just one obstacle, but many complicated ones all compressed together. Bad people, difficult and unfamiliar rules, and too many hasty decisions piled on top of one another and made the already complicated course that much more challenging. I was learning about corporate finance and capital formation, character judgment and the high cost of hurried decision-making very quickly, and very painfully. I needed to spend more time evaluating my options. I needed to take more time for study. And I especially needed more time to just grow up. But I was on a self imposed fast track that I learned later was making this journey more demanding. The obstacle course I had started out on had seemed much easier. That same course had taken on a new, more complicated and tricky face.

Somewhere in the back of my mind I kept hearing "Slow down!" I kept charging forward. This pace would take its toll on me physically, financially, personally. But the energy of an impetuous youth is a very strong force to resist. Perhaps if I had slowed down events might have unfolded differently. Facts and history later prove that things often happen for a reason. The Almighty was teaching me the hard way – closing a window but opening a door. Or vice versa. Time after time I was given second, third and forth chances. Providence intervened again and again. The lesson is: there are always options if you slow down, observe and analyze.

7

Opportunities: Feast, Famine or Failure

After the distracting whirlwind of disastrous events I finally returned my focus to the nuts and bold operations of the reservation system. After a few weeks of hard work, doors began to open. I was signing up new territories left and right and beginning to see the light at the end of the tunnel. The reservation system was beginning to make money. The original business concept was working despite what the old boys' club was saying. We had had trouble raising money and were turned down by scores of investors, so why was the company performing so successfully? Because the concept possessed first-rate basics: a strong business foundation with growth potential well linked to a targeted, responsive market.

This time of intense work was exactly what I and the business needed. I focused on streamlining the operations with the invaluable assistance of Ken. A busy college professor, Ken still found time to share his wisdom and experience to help us improve operations. Ken was a great teacher and explained in detail where thoughts, ideas and theories came from. He was an incredibly interesting man, and I was grateful for the energy and impromptu OJT he gave me and the business.

Necessity: The Mother of Invention

We added ten more locations and replaced a few of the early operators that could not keep up with the reservation demand. The operation was now a-buzz with activity and momentum. Then a major break came along. The single largest provider of rental car insurance went out of business. They insured our business so we were forced to immediately seek out another company. What a job this turned out to be! After a month of concentrated work I found another insurance carrier. But during this search process members of our franchise frequently asked if I thought about getting into the insurance business. They told me if we went into the rental car insurance business they would give us their business.

I began to do some research on the rental car insurance business and learned that congress was about to enact legislation that would dramatically affect the insurance industry. This legislation would also have profound positive effects on the rental car business.

In addition to insurance services, the franchisee group was requesting a host of other services such as: leasing, car purchase programs and co-op advertising, that we could expand into individual businesses. With all of these new ideas for expansion I began to put together a plan to vertically expand the company.

A few months later after I had studied and developed this new expansion concept I sat down with my father and Terry and told them I thought we were facing a good business opportunity. I presented a plan whereby we could offer everything from rental reservations to fleet leasing to rental car insurance. A detailed spread sheet demonstrated each service as a business and the profit to be realized. I detailed down to the penny what it would take to capitalize the operations. I had built a business plan that resembled an operations manual. My father and Terry were quickly convinced that this was an opportunity we needed to capitalize on ASAP.

At this same time I pointed out that that there was within this rental car business an even bigger opportunity awaiting our attention. The traveler that was making a reservation with us was also looking to make a hotel and airline reservation. Why not link this traveler to independent car rental operators, independent hotels and regional airlines as well?

My dad and Terry thought that this was a pretty big plan; maybe too big to take on all at once. It was a lot to launch. But I heard my inner voice confirming my belief that the fly, rest and drive concept was going to provide the continuing growth the company needed after we were done growing the car rental segment of the business. After more discussions Terry and my dad began to share my vision. And thus we proceeded to expand the business together.

Back on the Trail With New Partners

The profits generated from increased franchisee locations were going towards the little debt we had accumulated and to expand operations. From an operational stand point we were back on track. However, we still needed more capital in order to pursue the expansion and development plan. Personally, I was still reeling from the preceding months' disasters and was a little gun shy about getting back on the capital raising trail. But necessity breeds difficulties and even punishment sometimes, and I was going to have to take some more of both if we were going to move forward. So back out I went on the capital fundraising trail. This part of the obstacle course did not seem to have an end to it. And rather than me choosing this trail it seemed to be choosing me.

This time out on the trail things developed more quickly. Providence intervened again. A trip to Denver on behalf of the local franchisee led me to a meeting that put the company on a course to success. I met with a lawyer named Raul who was charismatic and blessed with almost inexhaustible energy. Although Raul was new to the securities law game he was very well connected politically, and he had an excellent understanding of what it took to take a company public. Raul had not yet been company counsel in a successful public offering, but he made up for this lack of experience with enthusiasm and stick-to-it-ness. We hit it off right away.

What a change from Sandy! Raul was a nice guy who was genuinely committed to the success of the company. Many years my senior, Raul had numerous friends in Washington D.C. because of his time working in the Carter administration. He was well spoken and well dressed, and he took it upon himself to teach me the finer points of corporate etiquette, including speaking and writing skills. Raul was a worldly guy's kind of guy.

One of the first things we did together was obtain a new investment banking firm. We also obtained a new Letter of Intent, the first step in taking a company public. Raul had a friend who introduced us to Ray in New York who in turn introduced us to the new underwriter. In a very short amount of time we were successful in obtaining an underwriter on Wall Street complete with a Letter of Intent. Ray was an enormous help and indicated he would assist us when the time came to commence the registration and syndication process.

Time had cost us money. We had had a few false starts that drained capital. The capital we had raised was used for the proper purposes, but if we were going to reenter the IPO process we were going to need more capital. This money would go towards the massive expenses of the IPO. Tom, a local stock broker, had heard about us through various circles. He had also seen a presentation I did on how our company was going to work. When Tom heard through the grapevine that we had obtained an underwriter he came forward offering his expertise and help.

Over the course of about six weeks Tom raised the much needed capital. Ironically, seven of these new investors were members of that old boys club that had previously scoffed at my proposal and rejected my investment invitation months before. I guess the good ole' boys finally began to recognize the solidity of our business plan, and my dogged tenacity to take this business public.

Public Offering: The Ultimate Goal, the Ultimate Challenge

And off to the races we went again! This time around we had a little more money in the bank. We did not need to raise as much capital as the first attempt because the reservation operation was up and running. Also my father said to "pull out all the stops" in order to get the offering done. He said he and my mother would help out as much as they could personally, and in addition we would use the profits from our other company as they became available.

The first tasks were to get an offering document together concomitant with getting our books and records audited by what was then one of the big five accounting firms. These were both big assignments, but now I was armed with an attorney who was behind the company and behind me. Getting the audit on track was very complicated. This was on the job training once again, and I had to learn about every aspect of corporate finance and going public as each step unfolded. I was simultaneously working with Raul on the offering document. Along with both of these tasks I was continuing to manage day to day operations at the office. I was putting in fourteen and sixteen hour days, but I was young and had plenty of energy. I loved what I was doing and on top of everything else I was now having a ball. The bees and naysayers had all gone away. Sandy was out of the picture, too. This time around everything felt different in a good way.

The new underwriter was young. His reputation was not the best but it was not bad either. He felt that with a little push we might very well get the offering off the ground. We started out with a good audit firm. The local partner was a charismatic and caring individual who helped raise some interim capital. His audit team was under orders to complete the audit ASAP. This was a demanding task for all of us. Even my father and Terry were involved. It was all hands on deck.

The audit process involved techniques and processes with which I was unfamiliar. The terminology was foreign. The interpretations by the auditors of my operations from a financial perspective were Greek to me. And the goal as I understood it was different for them. But what did I know? It was at this point I should have stopped and spent some time learning as much as possible about this very important process. I also should have questioned the intentions of the audit firm. In retrospect the best course would have been to educate myself thoroughly about accounting, auditing and the responsibilities and risks of this process.

I could have hired an outside consulting accountant to assist me through this very complicated process. I have since learned that hiring an accountant to watch over another accountant is a very valuable practice that can keep auditors from running amuck. Auditors can really get quagmired in their own rules and interpretations. As a result we get to suffer all kinds of delays, disclosures and derailment because of their over-zealous pursuit to cover their own butts. And all of this is at our expense. Hiring a consulting accountant can prevent this awful out of control audit nightmare.

Unfortunately the local partner we had begun to work with moved to California to another firm. The new guy was nothing like the partner we began with. He was a stick in the mud, with no personality and zero interest in the company or its well being. As far as he was concerned we really were not a client but a burden. I should have fired him right then and there. His only thought was to get this audit done and get out of there. He did not care about being the slightest bit proactive in the process.

What I did not know would have a very detrimental effect on the offering. The auditors could have given me a heads up on several of the issues they raised. But unbeknownst to me they were under orders from the new guy to just get the audit out as fast as they could, no matter the results. First we received a Qualified Opinion. This meant that they felt we could not sustain the business. The footnotes read like *War and Peace* with a little of the script from *The Towering Inferno* thrown in. The audit was an absolute disaster. All of this could have been avoided. To avoid the Qualified Opinion we could have been alerted by the auditors to put in a little more capital. We even had the needed capital! This would have eliminated the need for the long ugly commentary in the foot notes. Had the auditors simply provided us with more information, taken a little more time and care with our case, we could have moved forward.

The audit was incorporated into the formal registration document Raul and I were working on. The new guy gave our document little time and even less attention. He took shortcuts that really hurt us. When the document was done and ready for review by the underwriters counsel, it was an awful read. It contained very few elements that accurately and truly described what the company was all about. It focused on the poor condition of the company and the fact that the auditors had little confidence that the company would survive. The positive components such as our growth rate, profit margin, growing asset value, and increasing cash flow were totally omitted or ignored. The document reviewed by the underwriters counsel had no "good"; just the "bad and the ugly."

Following this dismal review the document was sent off to the underwriter's legal counsel. When you complete an audit you have a set number of days in which you can file with the SEC and receive clearance to sell your registered securities before you "go stale." If you go stale you have to re-file and start the entire process all over again.

Before we could file with the SEC we had to go through the underwriter's counsel's office. Enter Cruella, young, pompous, rude and condescending all wrapped up in one uptight and stiff physicality. Cruella knew we had a limited amount of time to file with the SEC, but she did not care nor was she the slightest bit concerned about our deadline.

Usually the underwriter's counsel turns a document around quickly and with few comments. Three weeks passed before Cruella informed Raul that she was very busy and would need more time on our document. Raul reminded Cruella about the SEC's ticking clock to which she responded that the deadline was not her problem or concern. Raul called Cruella everyday thereafter to push her to complete our case, but to no avail. I was on the phone to the underwriter as well, who supposedly was on the phone to Cruella. After five weeks with absolutely no response Raul and I decided to fly to New York and plant ourselves in Cruella's office.

Again, it bears repeating: when you hire an underwriter you also hire their legal counsel. Always confirm that the legal counsel is ready, willing and able to take on and complete the very demanding task of preparing an offering document. Interview the counsel who will be involved with your document at the end of the process. Make sure that the chemistry is good. If the two lawyers involved with your offering do not communicate well you have a formula for disaster. The obstacle course becomes a road full of land mines.

With the computer that contained our document tucked under my arm Raul and I flew to New York and set up shop in the underwriter's office. The underwriter wanted Cruella to complete her review as much as we did because he had paid a retainer that would not be returned. Or so he said. (We would find out later that was not truly the case.) After four unsuccessful attempts to set up an appointment with Cruella over the phone, Raul and I set off to park ourselves in her office.

At Cruella's office we greeted the receptionist and asked to see Cruella. The receptionist announced our arrival via intercom to Cruella. We sat down and waited. We waited some more. After two hours Cruella emerged in all her pompous glory and chastised us for coming unannounced. I was out of patience and good manners. I just let go and told her how unprofessional and rude she was to not respond to us for five weeks. I said she was careless and unprofessional to not heed the clock in this time sensitive process. Cruella's response was infuriatingly predictable: she would just have to work our case into her schedule. Then she turned her back and stormed off. What a *%#?!

We returned to the underwriter's office and gave him the news. He then got on the phone to Cruella's boss. The boss said he was very busy and that at the first opportunity he would discuss it with her. End of conversation. Now we were really shut down. We could not file the document with the SEC without the underwriter's council's approval. Cruella held all the cards. Ahhh!!!!!!.

Chapter Summary

Time is money in business. And bad associates and partners can cost a business both time and money. But perseverance and tenacity through tough times can reverse the damage done. Finding partners who are experienced and honest, and who bring energy to your business are as valuable to taking a company public as the capital needed to finance the undertaking. The success of each step in the public offering – getting the documents in place, the audit, the underwriter's review – all are inexorably tied to the individuals hired to do each task. Our story recounted thus far clearly illustrates how the right individual can move the process along, and the wrong individual can completely stymie and even derail the entire offering. The more you know about each individual working on your offering, the better your chances that the offering will move forwards with fewer road blocks. Ask around and even interview prospective auditors and underwriters.

8

New Obstacles Not Imagined

Finally, after two long, frustrating days of waiting at the underwriter's office Cruella emerged. We were summoned to her office for a meeting. Upon our arrival we were ushered immediately to a conference room. With her boss seated beside her Cruella then chastised us for the next thirty minutes. When it was my turn to speak I stated the obvious, again, about our deadline with the SEC that provoked a lot of concern and stress for me and my partners. Finally, the atmosphere in the conference room began to cool a bit and the real story behind Cruella's behavior towards us began to emerge: apparently the underwriter – our underwriter – owed Cruella's law firm a sizable sum of money.

Cruella's firm had witnessed several instances of poor performance by this underwriter in the past and did not believe he would be successful in getting our offering closed. Therefore they were reluctant to proceed with our offering which they believed had a very poor shot at an IPO. Cruella and her boss did not share all of these facts with us that day. They alluded to the situation and we later learned the details. Had we known then the extent of their concerns we might have moved on and found another underwriter. But during the meeting that day the decision was to move ahead and find a way to get the offering done.

In the next few days Cruella finally started to communicate with Raul. However, the communication was not very encouraging. She could tell by his work on the preparation of the registration statement that Raul was not very experienced. He did posses a good deal of charisma and was able to keep Cruella in the game. As time passed Cruella began to get the idea, the concept of what we were trying to do with our business. And guess what? She liked the concept and could see by our progress that it was in fact working.

Avoiding Derailment and Doing What We're Told

At this time a critical and portentous shift occurred in our case. Cruella began to bypass Raul and communicate with me directly. Over the course of several conversations she began to spill noxious potion about Raul. She lambasted Raul and said he was hurting rather than helping our offering. Cruella pointed out the poor quality of the document he had prepared. And then came the bomb: if the deal was to get done at all we would have to bring in another lawyer to redraft the registration statement.

I was shocked and so was Raul. But we really had no choice: if we wanted to proceed with the registration process we had to hire another lawyer. Raul, at his own expense, hired another securities lawyer to redraft the registration statement. In a few days the redraft was complete and we were ready to file.

The accountants were ready to begin but we noted a hesitance in the underwriters to proceed. This was to be a foreshadowing of things to some. We finally filed the registration statement after weeks of pushing, pulling and tugging with lawyers, accountants and the underwriter. Our timeline began to become critical. We were able to pull a few political strings in Washington that moved the process ahead. In a few weeks we were cleared to begin to sell and syndicate the offering.

I flew back to New York and met with the underwriter. He said it was time to start syndicating the offering and because I was very young and did not know about the ins and outs of an underwriting I needed a grey haired guy to help me in front of potential investors. Enter the grey haired guy we will call Scotty. I had suggested that we hire Ray to help but the underwriter said Ray had too much baggage and would not be as successful as Scotty.

This supposed expert Scotty was an enormous disappointment. He had the grace and manners of a warthog. Every sentence he spoke was laced with profanity. His physical appearance was not any better: there was continual butt scratching in front of every new introduction. And then he added insult to injury and offered to shake your hand. Gross! I was young and inexperienced but I knew bad manners when I saw them! This vulgar little guy and I did not hit it off at all. Scotty was rude and crude and yet believed he was the center of the savvy universe. I could not stand him. But this is what the underwriter ordered and so off we go.

The Pitch

We started with meetings in New York, several a day, one right after another. One of these meetings was with one of the Principals of a firm by the name of Grady Hatch, more about them a little later. By the end of the first week I was exhausted. Then on to Denver for more meetings and more presentations. After a while I started to get in a rhythm. The only decent thing Scotty ever said to me was that I was a quick study and a natural born pitchman. After the second round of meetings he told me "Kid you could get paid to do this for a living." Well, by now I knew the business. And I was, after all, passionate about what we were doing. I doubt I could have been as effective a pitchman with another business.

Although I really disliked working with Scotty, this experience taught me how to present a company to potential investors. This is a very important skill to learn. The key is to maintain the interest of the investor. The presentation must be to the point, concise and weave together the facts with the intentions of your business. You must be thoroughly versed in your numbers, demographics, accounting, shareholder dilution, and demonstrate that you know all the details of the structure of the deal you are presenting.

You only get one chance to make a good impression to investors and if you stumble the opportunity is gone. The guys on Wall Street see hundreds of deals a week. They make the decision to get in or out in a matter of minutes. You do not have much time and if they suspect you do not have your act together they will drop you like molten metal. Be quick and concise. Be well prepared, be direct and articulate. You are also the cover on the book so look neat and professional. And even if you don't feel confident, look and act confident.

These pitch meetings with out of state investment bankers and stock brokers ended with one big meeting back in Albuquerque. This large gathering, the big show, was held to mark the successful end of the syndication process and culminate in a closing of the offering. The meeting was held in a conference room with several dozen people including the underwriter. It went off alright except for the undercurrent caused by the underwriter and his professional baggage. As fast as I was convincing investment bankers and stock brokers to invest in us, the underwriter's reputation was knocking them off the radar. The investors loved the concept but felt the underwriter was incapable of closing the deal. The offering document also still did not read well and had something that caused investor concern: that Going Concern qualification.

I had now done my part. The days were growing short on the deadline and the allowable time before the underwriting expired by law. If all passed the deadline the entire process would have to begin again. Days of waiting turned into weeks and the underwriter could not verify the amount of money committed in the syndication. Ray's in-office manager Andy was overseeing the syndication. He was a great guy and Andy and I got on very well. In later years we became good friends. But when I first met him Andy was having trouble with the syndication. He called me and told me I needed to come to New York and meet with some people that could help our situation. There were only about three weeks left before the SEC deadline so off I went.

Andy set up a few meetings but to no avail. He did however introduce me to Chuck. Chuck made the whole trip worthwhile. Ironically, I was reluctant to even go to a first meeting with him. I did not think a talk with Chuck would go anywhere and believed this guy was just another Wall Street leach. But Chuck would change my professional life. Again, intervention from above. A window was about to close and a door was about to open.

Closing One Door, Opening Another

Chuck waited patiently for thirty minutes while I made my pitch and finished another meeting. I was not excited about meeting with Chuck and was very cavalier when I walked into the room where he waited. Chuck was a slight man, well dressed and blue eyed, smoking a cigarette. He greeted me and then began in a soft spoken manner to ask a plethora of pertinent and informed questions.

Chuck seemed to know a lot about the company already but I did my best to keep up with him. He had been listening and watching me go from pitch to pitch. After we talked a few minutes he asked if I would let him set up a few meetings with people he knew; see if he could dragnet them into the deal? I was more than a little surprised by Chuck's offer because he did not ask for anything, did not have his hand out like everybody else. Chuck's offer seemed very legitimate. I accepted his help and he got right on the phones. Within fifteen minutes Chuck had set up about five meetings.

Chuck introduced me to some real players. These guys had the wherewithal to get the deal done. They understood the concept and liked the business model. The three things they all kept repeating to Chuck was 1. The document needed to be re-done; 2. The underwriter needed to go away and 3. Boy could this kid pitch! Chuck's contacts basically said if the changes they suggested were done they would participate in the offering and go all in.

What a fix I was in. I could now see how the deal could really get done. But how was I going to do it? How would or could I walk away from the underwriter? If I abandoned Ray as the underwriter would my professionalism and loyalty come into question? Would my character come into question? And how could I abandon the deal as it stood?

Chuck was supportive. He knew and understood the tight position I was in, but reiterated that for the deal to get done we needed new, solid, capable and experienced players and the correct approach to telling the company story. Chuck was great throughout this very confusing time. He showed me who the real can-do people were on the Wall Street. Chuck also helped me become even sharper in the pitch department. He was a real helping hand. But for Andy I would never have met Chuck. Chuck was the first guy on Wall Street who really seemed to care about our concept. And through all of this process Chuck never mentioned what needed to be in it for him. He just said, "When the time is right I know you will take care of me."

The problems associated with changing the underwriter and rewriting the deal would soon solve itself. The clock was going to eventually run out. All we had to do was make the decision to either extend the offering with an amendment or abort with the current underwriter. The last forty-eight hours before expiration my father and I sat in his office and discussed the situation. It was either tell the underwriter he was fired and abort the deal, or re-file the registration statement for an extension and try and save the existing deal. My father had a quarter: he said, "tails we abort, heads we extend." He threw the coin in the air and down it came. We would extend. We both knew intuitively that this was the wrong decision. We kept on flipping that coin until we got the right decision. Abort! We called Chuck first and confirmed his interest and willingness to help. He was in. We called the underwriter and gave him the news he was out and we were going to abort.

Chapter Summary

Thus a new episode began. Years later my father would have that quarter gold plated to remind us of that day. It also reminds me of how my father supported me in the most difficult of times. That quarter marks a happy, red letter day and the turning point on the obstacle course away from a very harrowing series of adventures.

Even though I was not successful with the offering I came away with many new tools in the tool box. I had learned more in that past year than I could have learned in four years of college. This was OTJ training in the truest sense. I had learned the basic rules of the public offering process, as well as the basic rules of Wall Street and the difference between the real and the phony players. And I had learned the skills needed to present a deal to investors.

I considered this my dry run. There was so much to learn. Now I felt better prepared for the next part of the obstacle course.

9

Controlled Crash Landing

Several things needed to be done in order for Chuck to do his part of the offering. First we needed a new audit without so many disparaging footnotes. Next we needed to re-write the registration statement and better tell the company story. I went back to Raul with the new plan and explained who all the new players were and how this time would be different. Always supportive and willing, Raul gave the go ahead and was in. I then met with the accountants. This time I came armed with knowledge and from the start laid out exactly what we needed from them. They agreed. Now back to the drawing board.

Chuck was busy getting a new underwriter in place and we were busy expanding the company's reach and tending to our daily upkeep. All in all things were moving along in our favor. We did however need some cash to pay for the expenses to file the registration statement for the new offering. Chuck was close to securing a qualified underwriter and said he would be back with us soon. We were not in any hurry as we had a lot on our plate. I was adding more locations to the network and was about to make two decisions that would change the course of the company. I would soon hire a right hand, Kyle; and I was ready to expand the business and provide insurance to the network members for their rental cars.

Kyle was a young college graduate from the local university business school. I needed someone who could follow my lead, a wingman so to speak. Kyle fit the ticket: he was young, energetic and eager to learn. I taught him to make presentations, and how to identify and sell new affiliate locations. Kyle brought to the job valuable knowledge obtained in business school, particularly pertaining to marketing. Kyle was an excellent addition to our company team. He was a hard worker and was willing to take on any task. I was focused on the corporate finance agenda, and Kyle took on the operational side of the business. We worked long hours for little money and we were getting a lot done. Unfortunately, Kyle would eventually prove to be a major mistake and become quite toxic to the business. But I will talk more about Kyle in the next book.

Risk vs. Opportunity

As mentioned earlier, many of the franchisees were encouraging us to get into the insurance business. We recognized that this was an excellent business opportunity, especially since the biggest player in the industry had recently stopped providing insurance to independent rental car companies, our primary market for expansion. I discussed this situation again with my father and Terry and we all agreed there was an opportunity here. But we also agreed that we did not have the money to move forward and capitalize an operation like this. However, through some recent contacts I had made I believed I had found a company that could provide the coverage for our affiliates on an exclusive basis. We could make a little money as the middle-man. Everyone liked this idea and I started to put the plan into action.

I met with Bob, the president of a Texas insurance company, and after a few visits we were on the verge of putting the new insurance product to work for our franchisees. Bob was a real player in the insurance business. He considered himself a rogue and a risk taker, and said, "I am the Lloyds of Texas." Bob took a liking to me and during the course of our meetings taught me what he knew about the risk finance industry. A good and intelligent person, Bob would help smooth out this section of the obstacle course by guiding us into a new and complicated business that would allow us to make money. Bob mitigated the risk of our new venture with his learned intervention. Over time, Bob would become a real asset to the company.

The new insurance venture Bob helped us put together promised big bucks for the company, and a much needed re-charge to our capital battery. I called Chuck to give him the good news. My news was met with a sigh and silence. Chuck did not seem nearly as excited as we were. In fact, he seemed distracted. I pressed for the reason for his lack of enthusiasm. Chuck said, "Kid, there is a lot on my plate right now. But do not worry it will all work out just fine."

The day after the not very satisfying conversation with Chuck, Chuck called me back. He said, "It just dawned on me what this could mean…the insurance and all. I get it, and it's great kid. You really have something there." I was relieved that Chuck finally got it. And Chuck had some very good news of his own to share. He wanted my father and me to come to New York and meet with the new underwriter, Steve. For the first time in a long while I could see light at the end of the obstacle course tunnel. I ran into my father's office to see when he would be available to travel. He said, "Let's go tomorrow!" That was a little too soon. We scheduled the trip for the upcoming weekend and went by way of Denver where we met with Raul.

Back on the Road

During out meeting with Raul in Denver we planned our presentation to the new underwriter, Steve. After celebrating at a Bronco's game the three of us climbed on the plane for New York. We checked in late at the hotel and went right to sleep in preparation for our Monday morning meeting. I woke up the next morning feeling like someone had put lead in my stomach and sand in my head. I was really sick with food poisoning. The Bronco game had given me more than just athletic entertainment – cold sweats, chills and the trots. What lousy timing! Thank God my father was in New York. There was no way I was going to make the meeting. He would have to go in my place and do the pitch. Although I had done the pitch hundreds of times, my father may have done it once. And he knew little about the corporate finance side. But being the true Simper Fi Marine he was and is, he said he would handle it, and went out to the meeting. All I could do was lie there in misery and wait.

Raul and my father returned to the hotel a few hours later. They were on cloud nine. Chuck had been a great help and Steve loved everything he heard. A Letter of Intent would be in our hands in a day or so. The bonus to this already good news was that Steve had offered to raise some bridge capital to cover the expenses of the offering. I was ecstatic. My father was very pleased that he had delivered a homerun for the business at a crucial time. And Raul was happy because we were working with a real underwriter, and we were involved with forthright people with good and honest intentions. Even though I was still feeling under the weather from the food poisoning I felt great! We were really getting somewhere.

I stayed another night in New York and recovered. The next morning Chuck arranged another meeting with Steve. Steve was a diminutive man with a vigorous smile and a commanding presence, and we hit it off immediately. Steve did most of the talking during our first meeting – about timing and the overall plan to take the company public. This kind of straightforward talk was unlike anything I'd heard before from an underwriter. The public offering process had always been on my shoulders. Chuck really delivered on this one. I left the meeting with a sense of confidence in my underwriter and in the process not known before. Chuck said, "Kid your deal is all but done. A few more things and we can tie a bow on this one." He was certain we would succeed. In spite of everything we had gone through, I could not help but believe we would succeed this time, too.

We went back to Albuquerque to tend to all the knitting that needed to be done. We were a few weeks away from completing the new audit. The underwriter's counsel was in contact very quickly with Raul and they got along famously. There was no tension between the two like there had been with Cruella. Raul and the new counsel could not do enough for one another. The document was soon ready and awaited the audit numbers.

Steve flew me back to New York a week later to make presentations to some of his investors. A few days later bridge money was in the bank. We had the dough to proceed full steam ahead. I could not get over the speed and effortless fluidity with which the entire process was moving forwards. The auditors were soon done and we were ready to file once again. Everyone in the company could feel the positive flow of events and could finally see the finish line.

A Few Last Obstacles

Chuck called me three days before we were to file. His voice was soft and low. Almost a whisper. He said, "Kid the NASD is going to close Steve down. You have lost your underwriter. But give me twenty-four hours and be ready to come back to New York. You will need to be in front of a new underwriter. It will be someone you know and who already likes you and your deal. Do not panic. I have it under control."

Those words landed on me like a tsunami. Chuck talked about a host of other things but nothing else penetrated my stunned brain. I was shocked, speechless. Déjà vu? Is this the way it was always going to be? Was I always going to be ten horses away from grabbing the brass ring? Was the obstacle course nothing more than an endless road through defeat and disaster? I was speechless, catatonic, utterly and completely deflated.

Now I had to tell my father and Terry. I knew it was going to crush them. It crushed me but I had had Chuck's calm, controlled delivery to get me through the news. My delivery of this bad news would be raw and emotional. I called them together and shared the details of my conversation with Chuck. They were as stunned and speechless as I had been. I told them it would be a couple of days before Chuck would get back to us on identifying a new underwriter. We all sat in silence for about five minutes. I am sure all the confused emotions I was feeling were running through them as well.

Partners Worth Waiting For

We were all sitting in this depressed silence when the office intercom went off and we were told Chuck was on the phone. He hadn't waited even twenty-four hours to call back, but just a few minutes. I was relieved thinking that now Chuck was going to help soften the blow to my father and Terry. We put him on the speakerphone. The first thing he said was "Men, do not worry." He then explained in more detail how Steve had lost money in some sizeable trades that did not go in his favor. There were also some people that owed Steve for a big stock purchase. Hence Steve did not have enough capital to meet the minimum requirements set by the NASD. Because he could not come up with the money needed in time he was out of business.

Chuck went on to say that he had another underwriter, someone that I had presented to before and liked me and the deal. Chuck told me I needed to be in New York by tomorrow night for meetings the following two days.

Relief and panic hit me at once. I was staring over another cliff on the obstacle course with unknown and uncontrollable forces dominating my progress. Again I was going to have to start from scratch. The next day, I was off again to New York. I felt like a yoyo toy. Up and down, in and out, back and forth. I was dizzy from the recent events. But like my father had taught me, I kept going. Never say die.

In New York I met with Bob from Grady Hatch. I had met

Bob before back when I tried to get the offering closed with my first underwriter. A tall, handsome, silver-haired man with a New York accent and a big grin, Bob was a gentleman. After I made my pitch Chuck went into high gear. He assured Bob that we had the entire deal syndicated. I had a following from the first attempt and Chuck had some new players that wanted into the game. Together this represented not only enough to close the initial offering, but enough to assure some strong and active aftermarket trading. Bob agreed with Chuck's analysis and was in. We had a Letter of Intent the next week.

Chuck had set up additional meetings with a host of other real players during the same trip to New York. Pitch after pitch, I gave it all I had. We generated commitments on the syndication one by one. I made a few calls myself to some of the people I had met with and interested in the first go-round. They received this presentation with open arms and confirmed they were in. We were putting together the syndication by the book. This was the way it was supposed to be done.

The Hot Deal

Chuck told me we were starting to heat the deal up a bit, and started the buzz about the deal already being done. Everybody wants in on something hot. Even though we had lost Steve and had some setbacks, we showed the Street that we were in position to file the registration statement. Grady Hatch had stepped in on a deal that was already done in a sense, and the Street ate it up. Meeting after meeting brought in more commitments. Chuck and I were turning out to be quite a good team. We had a good chemistry and people could sense it. Chuck had impeccable timing and was experienced in the art of getting a deal done. I had unbridled enthusiasm for our company, and time tested perseverance that kept me committed to the obstacle course until the public offering was successfully completed. In a few short days, we were back on track. Now we had to focus on getting through the rest of the registration process and the SEC.

The audit was ready. Steve's securities lawyer stayed on as new underwriter's counsel for Grady Hatch. That made the entire process much easier and smoother, and we were in registration a week after we signed with Grady Hatch. Again we used our political connections in Washington to move the registration a little faster. We were just about at the last round of comments when Chuck called and said we all needed to be back in New York for the big show he had planned. He confirmed that all of our committed investors were still in, and even more investors had now committed. Chuck said this will be one hell of a big show.

We climbed back on a plane and returned to New York yet again. Looking back at the events of the last year I felt like we had executed and survived a controlled crash landing. The ups and downs of this ride and physical and emotional toll of this part of the obstacle course were really beginning to show in me. I was running out of drive but I had so much riding on this journey I knew there was no turning back after all everyone had done.

Once back in New York I had to again pitch the company with all I had. I could not possibly go through this process again so this time it all needed to stick. This was the pitch of a lifetime. Everything needed to go right this time around. I visualized the underwriter doing his part. I visualized Chuck and me successful, and the offering closed. The offering could not fail at any cost this time. My emotional fuel tank was empty. There would be no more take-offs and no more controlled crash landings for any of us. This was it. This needed to be it this time.

Chapter Summary

This part of the obstacle course was very unnerving and frightening because there was an undercurrent that we had lost control. New and unforeseen obstacles were popping up at every turn. It was taking so much out of each of us we began to wonder if we would ever get this monster called our company under control.

As I look back I understand that everything happens for a reason. But at the time, whilst in the middle of the adventures and misadventures surrounding our public offering, I could not say I understood what the reason could be behind all of our difficulties. I did not know why the course was constantly shifting and moving under my feet, why I always felt off balance and in the dark. All I knew was there was a lot riding on everything I was doing. Everyone was counting on me to come through. The pressure was immense. I had no one to really talk to about how I was feeling, my insecurities and doubts. About how I often felt like I was just going to implode.

During a stressful period in a business startup it is important that we maintain our activities and relationships away from the office. It is also important to keep our families together. We need to allow ourselves time away from what can be consuming professional pressures, time that can refocus and recharge our emotional batteries. And time out from the office gives us a fresh perspective on what we are doing, strengthens our ability to make sound decisions and keep up with a demanding emotional pace. Never lose your touch with the outside non-office world, especially the world of your family. Nothing is more important.

10

The Last Pitch

We were preparing a bang up presentation for the Big Show in New York. Slides, handouts and small give-away gifts were going to be part of the presentation. Chuck hired a friend to hone my pitch, and we worked out details and changes long distance via the telephone. There was a buzz of activity around the office as we prepared for the biggest moment of our professional lives. I started to feel the pressure. We all did. There was a ton at stake.

Once again, I packed for what I believed was our last trip to New York. From the moment we landed my father, Terry and I were schooled on the do's and don'ts of what to say, who to say it to, and when to say it. Chuck's hired expert drilled, grilled and retooled my pitch over and over again. After a few days of this intense rehearsal I was numb. But I understood that this was this was the performance we'd been working towards for two years. I had to get it right.

The night before the Big Show I practiced the pitch over and over again into the wee hours of the morning. It all became a blur. I could not remember one pitch from another. At around one am I finally went to bed absolutely exhausted.

The Final Obstacle: Using the Skills & Tools

The next day I was up and ready. The event was planned to begin at five o'clock. Throughout that day I made a few short presentations to people who were important but were unable to come to the evening show. These were short and sweet, as Chuck did not want to wear me out. After lunch Chuck tucked me away in my hotel room where I was spared all of the confusion surrounding the last minute details of Big Show. I was able to remain focused and relaxed, although I kept going over the new hardened pitch in my mind. I remembered and practiced what Coach Brown had taught me years ago about visualization and the game, and reviewed the event to come on my inner movie screen, with positive results. I could hear Gino say, "See it like a movie in your mind kid!" Finally, the car came for me around four o'clock. I felt exactly like an athlete going to a big game. My adrenalin was flowing. I felt confident. I felt ready.

The next hour or so was a blur. I walked into the restaurant where we had reserved the meeting room. Everything was set up and in place. There were already a few people in the room but I sat down in quiet corner away from the growing crowd where I could move into my mental zone.

I needed to focus. I needed to collect myself for the best pitch of my life. I was a nervous wreck, but I remembered what I had been taught by my various teachers and began to visualize how I was going to present this pitch. Over and over in my mind I saw myself giving the pitch exactly as Chuck's hired hand had schooled me. I thought about Coach Brown, too, and how important visualization was in sports and in life. I was applying all of these lessons at a critical time in my career.

After a few minutes of focused visualization I walked back in the meeting room. There was food set out, a bar, the slide projector for the presentation, and the handouts and give-a-ways. The room was filled to overflowing with investment bankers and investors. There was a positive buzz in the air. Everyone was waiting with anticipation to hear about the company from New Mexico that almost wasn't; the company that had tried a number of times to get an offering off but had thus far failed.

What made this attempt feel so different? The professionals involved with our preparation. Their guidance and our tenacity to keep at it until we got it right had brought this deal to closure, and brought a mass of interested and sincere players to this presentation. Finally, the company was receiving the attention it deserved and needed.

The company, Chuck, my father, Terry and myself had all worked to get here, worked hard to amass a team of real people interested in seeing the company achieve the next level. I could feel the positive energy pulsing in the room. The deal was finally going to happen. The offering was going to close. We would be a public company with a few million dollars in the bank. We could finally execute the business plan the way it was supposed to happen. This time it was for real.

After a short introduction by Bob I was on. I breezed through the pitch. Everything unfolded in that presentation just as I had visualized it...smooth, to the point and confident. No one in that room was privy to all the details of what we had been through, but many knew that our being here at all was some kind of Wall Street miracle. With the possible exception of my father and Terry, maybe Chuck and Raul, too, no one knew that under my smooth, confident exterior I was scared to death! What a strange mixture of thoughts and feelings paraded through me that evening: scared, confident, relieved, and exhilarated. I had one really overwhelmed and confused head. Behind that podium my knees were quivering like grass in the wind, but thanks to all of the good coaches and teachers who had helped me through the obstacle course, my nerves and anxiety did not show.

My presentation and pitch received a short round of applause. After I answered a few questions from the crowd, Bob came forward and said it was time to relax and invited everyone to visit the bar. There was another round of applause and I was done. The people in the room immediately clustered around Bob, Chuck and me. Everyone wanted to know how much of the offering was available. The answer was none of the offering was available! It was all gone before we even came into the Big Show. The people in the room pushed at us hoping to get even a small piece of the initial offering. But we had nothing to give. They would have to get it in the aftermarket. This made the deal even hotter. We were officially on fire.

Chuck, my father, Terry, Raul and I went out after the Big Show and had dinner. Chuck looked at me across the table of a fine restaurant and said, "Kid, in a few days your deal will be done. We can tie a bow around this one. You made it."

With the exception of the auditors, the rest of the offering was pretty much automatic. At the last minute the auditors held us up. There was a few thousand dollars left to pay on our bill. The head partner said that if we did not pay the balance they would not give us the letter needed to clear the SEC and close the offering. What jerks! They knew we would have more than enough money to pay them in a few days but they wanted it right then. After all we had been through this was a relatively insignificant obstacle on the course. We had just enough in the bank to pay our bill. I delivered the check with the following message: "You will be the first people I fire when this deal gets done."

The End of the Obstacle Course

The letter from the auditors went off to both lawyers and within forty-eight hours the stock was trading at a premium. After another forty-eight hours the money was in the bank and we went back to New York for the closing party.

After all expenses were paid, we were handed a check by the underwriter's lawyer for over two million dollars. The brass ring! The lawyer had the check enlarged to the size of a bathtub and we all gathered around that massive check in Chuck's office and took a million pictures. We were all smiles: smiles of joy and relief. I choked up at one point when all that we had been through flooded my mind, sort of my own post traumatic stress. Ten rolls of film later, we were done at Chuck's office. We all went out to lunch as the guest of a major bank. What a change! Someone was courting us! They wanted our business. They wanted to know how they could get involved in helping the company to grow. What a feeling!

Acknowledging the Team Effort

The closing party was at Giraffes, one of the best restaurants in New York at the time. Our party took up the entire second floor. Everyone was there: wives, families, Raul, Chuck, Bob and the professional crew that made the offering possible. We had the time of our lives. I made a small speech that night and I thanked everyone who had made our success possible. It was never about one person. Our success as a business was the result of the good efforts by everyone who became involved in that last offering. These people were truly sincere in their desire to make the company a success. And I thanked them for their loyalty, professionalism and contributions that evening.

I thanked by my father for his ongoing support through many tough times. I thanked my wife for her words of encouragement and comfort and for her infallible confidence in me that enabled me to take on this risky business at all. I recounted how my mother believed in me enough to loan me money during the business' worst crisis. I thanked my partner Terry who kept the business functioning from the start, and Chuck and Raul who saw the potential and provided a much needed push at crucial times. And last but not least I thanked Bob who stepped in when most others would not and provided a turning point at the final step. It was so clear to me that night that getting through the obstacle course had been a team effort.

Chapter Summary

At the end of the obstacle course, we had a lot to celebrate. We had survived and prospered in spite of many, many difficulties: the dead weight we had dragged around, the nasty, even subversive individuals that had tried to derail our progress, the lost opportunities. We had all borne the expense of this process financially and emotionally, had endured the pain of near failure, and suffered the stress of running out of money and near collapse again and again. There were all those cross country trips, the endless rounds of presentations and pitches, the undercurrent of tension that comes from never knowing if the next attempt is going to run aground.

Getting to the closing party in New York marked where we had been and where we were going. This was the finish line for a long obstacle course filled with travails and tests in unknown territory. There was nothing like the sheer exhilaration experienced at the final closing. We had made it; we had achieved a major life changing goal.

11

In Review &
The Road Ahead

When I think back about the events of my first public offering it is with mixed emotions. I recall all of the mistakes, the wrong turns and dead ends, and the moments of amazing and saving grace that culminated in the final triumph. I am grateful for the good guys who helped me through the tough times. And I remember the bad guys who undercut our best efforts and delayed our progress. Well, they got theirs. Some were run out of business. Some even went to jail.

I also think about the closing party – everyone who was there and the great time we had celebrating our success. I look at all those pictures we took and remember the happy looks on everyone's faces that evening. Even though it was a difficult and challenging process, there are many good memories. And that sense of exhilaration when we knew the deal was finally done: there is nothing like it.

I learned so much during this process it is hard now to imagine how I was able to absorb it all. My experience starting a business taught me a few basic principles that I now live by. I spoke about them at the beginning of this book but they cannot be repeated too often: You begin with a plan. You implement your plan by building a team of people who you trust and respect, and who believe in your plan. You learn about your business from every possible source. You listen to your intuition and to your advisors, and learn to recognize and seize opportunities. You adjust your plan continually, and remain flexible throughout the process that unrolls before you like an obstacle course. And you always prepare for the unexpected because the unexpected is the foundation of the obstacle course.

The obstacle course tests you in ways you cannot imagine when you start out on this journey. It will exhaust you emotionally and fill your mind with doubt. It will put barriers in your path that look insurmountable, and push you to new highs and through even newer lows.

The Basic Rules

There is no clear or singular path through the course, only a few basic rules to follow and helpful tools to use while you are on it. These basic rules include:

Commit yourself to the course and be unwavering with your decision. Stepping forward and making the commitment to start your own business is the single most important decision you will make. And this decision must include your spouse's commitment to the business as well.

Visualize positive outcomes. Visualization is an acquired skill that should become part of your daily routine because this practice clears the mind and helps you manifest your intentions and reach your goals. Visualization is one of the most important tools at the startup of a business and throughout its development and growth.

Throughout every step of the process listen to your inner voice. Remember to heed your intuition, to follow your gut instinct. Your gut will guide you every time. The inner voice has only one purpose – to direct you to those things that serve your best interests – and that voice, which is your intuition, will always influence you correctly. Heed the inner voice.

Choose your partners carefully. At the very startup of a company set boundaries and establish rules about how you will work together. Your partners must complement your skills and also be able to take the reins when you cannot. Your partners must be people who trust your intuitions and decisions, and who you, in turn, trust without reservation. Mutual respect and trust among partners who recognize the importance of their role in the company are key ingredients to a successful business team.

As you develop your business plan analyze the risks and opportunities inherent in the enterprise. And keep analyzing these risks and opportunities with your partners and advisors as the plan unfolds. This may prompt further evaluation of individual commitment among the team members, including you. If you are not committed one hundred and ten percent, it's time to step back and re-evaluate the business plan. Your commitment to the business will be tested over and over again. That's part of the process, part of the obstacle course. If the commitment is sincere and is grounded in a foundation made of good, informed decisions that reflect your truest desires, then you will endure the ups and downs of the process. Looking back at my own experience it was my commitment to the business and my gut instinct about our plan that kept me going forward even when the odds seemed very much against success.

Value Life Away from the Business

Starting a business demands our full attention. The ups and downs can consume us. At times during the two years I spent creating the business and then taking it public I was so hyper-focused on the office that I lost track of many of my friends. My relationship with my wife and with my family was put on the back burner. I lived and breathed the new business, and gave up outside interests and hobbies. But I was young. I know better now, and advise others to avoid this kind of hyper-focus and tunnel vision on business matters to the detriment of your personal life. I have since learned that this sort of manic focus on the business is actually detrimental to my ability to make good decisions. I was stuck in my own mind, thinking about just one thing, blocked from access to new energy and fresh perspectives. I couldn't meet my own goals when I was unable to recharge my mental and emotional batteries, but I was too inexperienced to see how I was drained. I needed a tune up, which only comes from time out from the office.

In the years since that first business startup I have learned how to maintain both a healthy personal life and a successful professional life simultaneously. I strive to be a good businessman, a good partner, a good friend, a good son and a good husband. Whether overseeing a current business or starting a brand new company I do not disconnect with friends, my wife and family, or give up outside interests and hobbies. It is important to me as a professional and as a private individual to maintain a connection with the non-business world of people and activities. I no longer let business interrupt these aspects of my life because it is these very relationships and activities that get us through the difficult times at the office. We need to get away so that we can hear our inner voice and remember exactly what it is we want to visualize and work towards.

Looking Ahead: New Ventures, New Opportunities

Since that glorious, terrible, exciting, exhausting first business I have been involved in many new ventures. I have made mistakes but thankfully, have not repeated the mistakes told in this story. And just as with my past mistakes I have learned bundles from my new mistakes! Not all of my other business ventures have been successful. But I have learned as much from the unsuccessful ventures as from the successful ones. There are many important lessons to be shared and stories to be told in upcoming books.

Happily each new business venture has been a little easier to get off the ground than the previous one. Experience, even gained from difficulty, brings many rewards. It is easier now to recruit a new business team, and to select partners with precisely the skills needed to move the venture forward. It is a little easier to see beyond the difficulties of the present obstacle course, to look ahead, to hold the vision of completion and success. Most of all the adventure of a new enterprise has become a little more fun each time out. There is nothing as rewarding as building a new business, employing people and giving them new opportunities. There is nothing as satisfying as molding new management and encouraging and developing young talent. It is a very gratifying profession, enabling others to achieve their dreams, and is the reason I am still in the business today.

I encourage anyone with a vision and sense of calling to enter the obstacle course and begin your own business. But enter it knowing the risks and proceed with caution and with your inner voice activated. As demonstrated in my story there are personal and financial risks, and emotional and familial challenges inherent to the process. We cannot eliminate these risks encountered on the obstacle course. But we can arm ourselves with knowledge about the risks that can mitigate potential costs and difficulties. Sometimes new ventures moved forward smoothly, unhindered by obstacles and roadblocks. I chalk this up to two things: experience and luck. And even when the plan is unfolding easily, we always expect the unexpected.

Every time I look back over the journey recounted in this book my feelings are a different combination of good and not so good. But the one feeling that persists after all these years is regret. Regret seems to pop up more often than others. Why? Because I lost a dear friend, Terry. The business strained our relationship and we went our separate ways in an unsatisfying and none too conciliatory fashion. As I stated earlier, there were no boundaries or expectations in our business relationship, and this caused our friendship to fade and ultimately become non-existent.

I see Terry from time to time and when I do I remember the good times and what a gift he was to the startup and the beginning of my business career. I regret that our friendship became a casualty of the metamorphosis the company experienced as it grew. Our friendship just could not take that kind of prolonged strain and it finally broke apart. I regret the loss of this friendship very much. My relationship with my father was also tested in the business environment. Fortunately our friendship survived the professional pressures, and the trials and tribulations of our business ventures actually brought us closer together.

Over seven years, with the energy and commitment of many professionals including Terry and my father, my first business venture prevailed. During that time I actually started six businesses. Each of these enterprises – the rental car, hotel and reservation systems, an insurance company, a fleet leasing company, and a systems control – functioned independently and were all for a time quite successful. These ventures eventually led me to establish my corporate finance consulting and merchant banking firm, B.H. Capital Ltd. that is my primary business today.

In my next book I will share with you the obstacle courses undertaken with these business ventures. Although I had experience to draw upon, each new business had its unique set of problems and solutions. No two startups are the same. I had to discover and use new methods and tools to get through each new obstacle course. And I learned that the obstacle course can be very costly in ways not measured simply in dollars and cents. These costs are off the P & L and can be subtle and very complex. My next book will suggest how to cope with these perplexing costs.

The members of the key group that assisted me on my entrepreneurial venture changed over the years. New players that did not serve the business or who tried to take advantage of the company came and went. The company ultimately morphed into a different animal and its management team changed and even disbanded as different priorities emerged and corporate needs changed. I learned that over time everything - people, opportunities, our own needs - undergoes transformation. This is all part of the journey down the obstacle course. I learned to adjust my vision, realign my intentions and modify my goals to accommodate and profit from these inevitable changes. These subsequent journeys into new business territories will be elaborated upon in my next book. Until then, I hope my experiences recounted herein will shed light on your own professional journey, and give you courage and a sense of camaraderie during the tough parts of the obstacle course you find yourself upon.

Further Reading

Allen, David, *Getting Things Done: The Art of Stress-Free Productivity* (Penguin, 2002)

Bull, Steve, *The Game Plan: Your Guide to Mental Toughness at Work* (Capstone, 2006)

Gawain, Shakti, *Creative Visualization: Use the Power of Your Imagination to Create what You Want in Your Life* (New World Library, 2002)

Schultheis, Patrick J., *The Initial Public Offering: A Guidebook for Executives & Boards of Directors* (Bowne, 2004)

CPSIA information can be obtained at www.ICGtesting.com
Printed in the USA
LVOW130404111212

310836LV00004B/6/P